DEATH

IS NOT

The End

Turning the Chains of Grief into

PEACE, POWER, AND PURPOSE

For a New Day

By

NATASHA HARRIS-TATE

TABLE OF CONTENTS

FOREWORD

This book was not born out of theory. It was born out of love, loss, and a journey no one ever truly prepares for. Before these pages became words, they were tears. Before they became encouragement, they were moments of deep sorrow. Before they became hope for others, they were anchored in the life of a man who meant everything to me—my husband.

My late husband was more than a spouse. He was a devoted husband. He was a loving and present father. He was a faithful Pastor who gave his life to serving God and His people. He walked in integrity. He led with compassion and loved with a strength that covered our family. His love touched everyone who encountered him. His life reflected purpose. His prophetic voice carried wisdom, encouragement, and truth. To me, he was my covering, my partner, my confidant, and my safe place.

His passing left a space that words cannot fully describe. The silence was loud. The absence was heavy. The grief was real. There were days when the weight felt unbearable. Questions outnumbered answers, and pain seemed to overshadow promise. Even in the depths of grief, I discovered that God was still present. Healing is not instant, but it is possible. Even in loss, purpose does not die.

Along this difficult journey, I have not walked alone. I am deeply grateful for my family, friends, and the spiritual leaders who stood beside me. They prayed for me, encouraged me, and lifted me when I did not have the strength to stand on my own. Your love, presence, and unwavering support carried me through one of the roughest seasons of my life. I will forever be thankful for each of you.

This book reflects that journey. It is my tribute to the man who loved me, led me, and prayed for me. It is also my testimony that grief does not have the final word. My husband's life continues to speak—through the lessons he lived, the love he gave, and the legacy he left behind.

My prayer is that as you read these pages, you will find strength where you feel weak. Find light where there has been darkness, and hope where there has been despair. I pray that you will come to know that healing is available. Joy can return, and your life still holds purpose—even after loss.

This book is for anyone who has loved deeply and lost painfully. It is dedicated to a man who will forever be honored, remembered, and loved. His life mattered. His love remains. His legacy lives on.

With Love,

— Pastor NaTasha Harris-Tate

"But thanks be to God! He gives us the victory through our Lord Jesus Christ."
— 1 Corinthians 15:57

CHAPTER 1

The One He Kept for Me

Just as it took Israel 38 years to finally rise up and be ready to enter the Promised Land, in the tapestry of my life, the threads of singleness were woven deeply into the fabric for thirty-seven long years. It was a pattern set early on, one that I followed with a heart full of faith. My childhood and adolescence were chapters straight out of a spiritual odyssey; where others had parties and extra-curricular youthful things to do, I had my steadfast companions: the church and my Bible. The lessons of my youth were clear and unwavering. To be single was not to be solitary, but to be wholly devoted to the service of the Lord's house. I was raised to believe that before one even considered marriage, their life ought to be a testament to caring for the things of God. And care I did, pouring my spirit into caring for the things of God and the local church, while striving to be a beacon of His light in every act of citizenship. I walked the path of Timothy, the young figure of the Bible who was told not to let anyone look down on him because of his youth but to set an example for the believers. By fifteen, I was not only following in Timothy's footsteps; I was ordained to lead the way for others, my sermons beginning years earlier, delivered earnestly to an audience of attentive dolls. As the pages of my life turned and I matured, I'll confess that my gaze did wander occasionally. The idea of someone noticing me, of being seen not just as a preacher but as a woman, was a whisper of a thought that I'd quickly hush. My friends now tell me, with a hint of amusement, that they saw me, admired me from afar, but I seemed to them a fortress of purpose, unapproachable in my resolve. God, it seemed, had fitted me with blinders, sparing me from what I might have deemed frivolous distractions. I wasn't immune to missteps, because there were times when the path I walked bent under the weight of repentance. Yet, through every trial and triumph, my mission never wavered – I was to be the Evangelist God called me to be. The vision of marriage, as depicted in Proverbs 18:22, lingered in the back of my mind – to be someone's "good thing." While some find contentment in solitude, my heart yearned for the chapters of life that included being a wife, a mother, and yes, continuing as a preacher of this great Gospel. My prayers to God were specific: a tall, dark, and handsome man with a dazzling smile, perhaps an athlete, who would dance in worship and not shy away from tears. As I navigated through my single years, I held these prayers close, trusting in God's timing, knowing that when He deemed it right, He would send me not just any companion, but the one tailor-made for me. And in the grand design of my life, every year of waiting, every moment of serving, was but a prelude to the love story that God had penned for me. In the quiet recesses of my heart, there bloomed a quiet determination—a recognition that the journey of self-love and self-improvement was not merely a path to another's heart, but a sacred pilgrimage to my own. I stood before the mirror of my soul and saw clearly the work that lay ahead. To be loved, one must be lovable, not in the superficial sense, but in the richness of spirit and character. I did not wish to be the half waiting to be made whole; instead, I aspired to be complete, a single entity worthy of love in my own right. With resolve as steadfast as the tree in Psalms 1:3, I labored on myself—at times harshly, guided by the deepest form of tough love. My prayers grew fervent and passionate. I sought a partner who could weather life's storms with me and stand firm on his own foundation. "Lord," I would say, "send me a man whose confidence lets him stand tall, so I never have to shrink to make him tall." This was my prayer—not just for a companion, but for a comrade, a co-warrior for God and His children. I envisioned a man who would help me as I would help him, building a synergy of strength and faith. Days turned into years. I found myself alone—not only in the physical sense, but in the rituals of life. Showers turned into sanctuaries where I whispered prayers for a husband I had yet to meet. I asked for divine hands to sculpt his spirit, to prepare him for our union. As calendar pages fluttered away, I watched others' milestones: weddings, anniversaries, and baby showers. I became the perennial guest, the eternal godmother, an emblem of celebration for others, always wondering when it would be my turn for matrimonial joy. Doubt crept in at times—a quiet thief questioning if singleness was a permanent fate. I wondered if my role was to be the ever-supportive friend, a spiritual mother to all, rather than a wife to one. I ventured into relationships: short flickers of hope that soon fizzled, never the grand love story I was meant to live. Despite moments of despair, my faith endured. I kept living a life that mirrored scripture, finding solace in my own company. There was grace in going to the movies alone, in answering, "Who are you dining with tonight?" with a smile and, "Me, myself, and I." Solitude brought peace, whether curled up with reruns or enjoying the silence of my own four walls. In that peace, I learned to cherish myself, to appreciate the beauty of my own company. Little did I know, this chapter of contentment was only a prelude. The prayers whispered in the shower would soon echo in another's heart. At 35—a number society ties to a ticking clock—I yearned for meaning, yet floated in fleeting affections. The phone rang, but those voices wanted thrills, not partnership. I was not made for flings; I yearned for something real. The world seemed to view my singleness as a challenge. Some men swaggered in, gambling who could unravel the 'mystery' of Tasha. To them, I was a riddle, a trophy, a way to prove I was not above anyone else, not as favored by God as others thought. I thank God for my upbringing. Raised by strong-willed women, I was schooled in discipline, integrity, and the stark divide between heaven and hell. This strict tutelage sculpted my initial view of God as a fearsome entity, one to be revered and feared in equal measure. I first sought Him out of a dread of eternal flames rather than love. Yet, as time unfurled like the petals of a blooming rose, so did my relationship with God. I discovered His warmth and grace, realizing that He was not solely a God of wrath but also of love. Even so, I lived my life feeling somewhat distant from others, always worrying that if I stepped out of line, I would bear the brunt of divine disappointment. I've often laughed when reminiscing about my youth, about how others could skip school with no consequence, yet I felt that if I so much as entertained the thought, my mother would somehow sense it. The idea of engaging in the recklessness of youth with men left me paralyzed by the fear of not just earthly consequences like pregnancy, despite precautions, but also the celestial fallout. God's displeasure was the one thing I couldn't risk. It wasn't that I fancied myself a perfect angel of virtue, despite the whispers and sidelong glances that suggested otherwise. "She thinks she's better than us," they'd say, or "She walks and talks like she's the living Bible." The truth was, I grappled with the same tempests that others did; I just navigated them differently. I was held back by the certainty that I would get caught and provoke God's anger.

From my earliest memories, I've been driven by a desire to make my Heavenly Father proud and to live in a manner that reflects His love and grace. It wasn't about being 'Miss Goody Two-Shoes'—it was about honoring the values that were instilled in me from the cradle. It was about being true to myself, to the unbreakable spirit within that no game, no challenge, no taunt could ever shatter. There was a time in my life, a chapter I recall with a mix of fondness and distress, when the mere thought of displeasing my father would send me into a spiral of self-reproach. I've seen others drift through life with a frightening ease, hopping from one relationship to the next, leaving a trail of broken connections without a backward glance. That was a dance I could never join, a melody that never matched my heart's rhythm. Perhaps it was the Holy Spirit that nurtured this conviction within me, this deep-seated need to make my Father proud. As a single woman, I walked a path lined with the same desires that whispered to others in the silence of the night. Did I not yearn for the gentle touch of affection, the warmth of companionship, just like anyone else? Of course, but there was a calling upon me that shaped my destiny – a leader I was meant to be, a mentor to guide others. The man destined for me, I knew, would share this journey, not perfect but aligned in spirit and in truth. I remember vividly, around the age of 35 or 36, the weariness that began to seep into my bones. The solitude that had once been my strength began to weigh heavily upon me. The saved, single, and sanctified gatherings lost their luster, and I felt an ache for the blessings of companionship I saw others rejoice in. It was during this time that my conversations with God took on a new depth. It was in this conversation that He challenged me, "What else can you do in the meantime?"

"In the meantime?" I questioned the words hanging between us like a promise yet to be unveiled. Yes, the meantime. That period God gifts us between the asking and the receiving, pregnant with possibility. God nudged me towards growth, towards education. I had a lot of dreams I had shelved away – certificates to earn, degrees to finish, a longing for the halls of Bible school, and a minor in Christian counseling. So, I made a pact with God: if He provided the means, I would pursue my education. Doors began to open, and soon I was immersed in learning and flourishing. My focus shifted from the roles I played in others' milestones to my own ambitions and progress. In the whirl of self-improvement, from bible classes to vacations, I found my 'meantime' filled with purpose. It was in this season of growth and introspection that September arrived, bringing with it a celebration – my mother's birthday back home in Harrington, Delaware. Unlike the subtle festivities of the South, the North often celebrated with revival meetings. I was to open the first night of the revival, a birthday jubilee in the guise of worship. It was the second night when fate quietly stepped in. As one of my closest friends preached, my eyes fell upon a young man in the audience, who was visibly moved by the message. I offered a silent prayer of thanks for the word being sown into his life, oblivious to the role he would soon play in mine. After the service, he approached me. He introduced himself as Tony, not as the Prophet, simply as a man who held my mother in high regard. Our interaction was brief, a polite and sanctified hug, nothing more. I did not linger on his presence, nor did I search for a ring upon his finger – such were the games of the heart I no longer played. The following day, over dinner, a friend inquired casually, "What do you think about Prophet Tony?" I couldn't place him, the man from the night before, until they reminded me. Little did I know that fleeting exchange was merely the prelude to a symphony God had been composing all along. In this chapter of my life, every trial, every prayer, every moment of patience was leading me to a crescendo of change. The meantime was coming to a close, and the next chapter was about to begin.

As I recall that day, it feels like a story plucked from the pages of a novel—the kind where you find yourself chuckling and nodding, thinking, "Oh, I've been there." I remember shaking my head emphatically, the word "no" tumbling out before I could even give it thought. "Why not?" he had asked, his curiosity piqued. "I think you two would be great together." But I was resolute, even if my reasons felt a tad superficial at the time. "He just... isn't my type," I said, fumbling for a gentler way to express that although he was handsome, he didn't match the list of requirements I had envisioned, nor did he possess the rich, chocolate hue I had prayed for. You see, I had this dream of a little dark-skinned child, a mini-version of me, to whom I could pass on the wisdom of self-love and the knowledge that our melanin was nothing short of exquisite. But this man, he was caramel-complected with curls that caught the light, and I stubbornly told myself, "No, this isn't what I asked for."

And so, I brushed the thought of him aside, like an inconsequential fluff of lint. But fate, it seems, had other plans. A week later, my inbox pinged with this message: "Hi, woman of God, hope you're having a wonderful day today." I replied with polite detachment, not giving the exchange a second thought. Yet, the very next day, there he was again, his message waiting for me, and this time, something stirred within. "Could it be?" I mused, "Is he... interested?" Our chats became a tapestry of daily rituals. Despite my efforts to maintain a safe distance, our conversations wove us closer together. It's a peculiar thing, praying for something fervently, and then, when it's finally before you, conjuring every excuse to turn away. I marveled at my own hesitance—

after years of longing for companionship, for a family, here I was, inventing reasons to reject what I had sought. He was different from my prayers, yes, but not in the ways that mattered. He wasn't tall or athletic; he was fairer than I'd imagined, and to top it off, he was a preacher—something I'd specifically thought I didn't want. "I'd rather have someone less... prominent in the church," I'd told God, half-jokingly. But it seemed God knew better; He knew I needed someone extraordinary. And extraordinary he was—a prophet with patience as I'd never seen, strength in his convictions, someone who could truly see NaTasha Cherelle Harris for who she was. Our conversations delved deep, and I remember testing him, throwing him the curveball of my independence and my refusal to ever be diminished by a man. His response? An unwavering, "That's great. I'm here for it." When I probed him on his bachelorhood, he replied with a line that was so disarmingly sincere yet playful that it caught me off guard, sparking laughter between us. It was in these moments, these exchanges, that I began to see the layers of the man before me. Time passed, and as he made plans to visit, reality set in. I made it clear—my roots were now firmly planted in the South, and I had no intention of moving back to the chilly climates of the East Coast. His answer was not what I expected; he didn't ask me to move. Instead, he spoke of biblical commitment, leaving me speechless with his resolve to "leave and cleave." Our relationship blossomed from there, with visits to each other's churches, meeting leadership, meeting friends, and eventually sitting at a round table where Tony faced a barrage of questions from my dearest allies. It was a moment straight out of a council scene in an epic saga, each friend playing the part of a wise advisor, assessing whether this man could indeed be the one for NaTasha Harris. And as I share this tale, it's with a smile, because life, I've learned, is the most unexpected of storytellers, and sometimes, the story it writes for you is even better than the one you had imagined. I remember one of the questions was, "My friend is stubborn, if she's mad enough," she said, "she won't so much as glance at her phone for weeks. How, pray tell, would you handle such a spirit?"

His answer was simplicity wrapped in conviction. "I know where she lives," he declared. "I'll call, I'll knock; she will hear me out." It was then that a spark ignited in my girlfriend's eyes—a glimmer of admiration, perhaps even the beginning embers of affection. "At that moment," she confessed, "I like him." This man of God had weathered the barrage of our tests, each crafted to unveil a flaw, a chink in his armor, to vindicate my doubts. Yet, with each trial, the chorus of our friends sang in unison, "We approve." Then came the day he resolved to propose. My heart, a tempest of uncertainty, urged me to retreat. "Please," I beseeched my mother, "tell him I'm not ready." He, with a ring already in his pocket, was discouraged. But my mother, sage as ever, counseled patience. "Tasha may run," she said, "but wait for her. It'll be worth every second." And so, he waited. In that season of waiting, I stood at the crossroads of singleness and union, nearly forfeiting the divine gift before me over a list of trivial, self-imposed rules. My pastor, ever the voice of reason, once quipped, "Who cares how he dresses? Once you're married, you'll pick out his clothes anyway." It was a gentle tease to remind me of what truly mattered.

The trivialities that once seemed monumental—his disinterest in gyms, his preference for quiet corners and books over the roar of sports crowds—faded into insignificance. What mattered was his love, steadfast and true, the kind that needed no shadows, no secrets. This man stood before me, dismantling my expectations, urging me to mature,and to embrace growth over a checklist. "You say you want a man of God? Then look inside," I reminded myself. "It matters not what's on the outside, but the inner soul that defines a person." And so, I taught my single sisters in our classes: "Before you dwell on the external, tell me of his heart, his spirit. For the true essence of a person always finds its way to the surface." With time, I saw his essence, his outer beauty, and his inner light, and it was radiant. Then, as the wheel of time turned, I was ready. "I can't face another New Year without you," I whispered. His response mirrored my own longing. The proposal, nestled within the blooming days of May on my birthday, was as sincere as his heart. And I said, "Yes." The courtship was brief but intense. September 2012 marked the beginning, and by April 2014, we were bound in matrimony. In our hearts, we knew—when you find the one ordained for you, time becomes a mere detail. April 26th, 2014, was etched into the stars as our day. As I walked down the aisle, serenaded by Maurette Brown Clark's soul-stirring melody, I knew it was the anthem of our journey. "The one he kept for me," the song promised, "until it was time." Once upon a time it seemed a phrase too fanciful for the likes of me, a woman whose heart had weathered thirty-seven winters. Yet, there I was, poised at the threshold of a moment that felt ripped from a storybook, with its pages worn from the turning of time. I found myself stepping into a scene that was both a culmination of years and a gateway to eternity. My feet graced the aisle like a whispered promise, gliding towards the man who was my answered prayer. The church—my grand cathedral of dreams—was a tapestry of faces, hundreds of souls that made the walls seem to pulse with life. Fifteen bridesmaids, in a parade of elegance, mirrored fifteen groomsmen, who Tony had rallied like a general mustering his finest soldiers. Our flower girls sprinkled petals as if sowing seeds of joy for our future, and our ring bearer, small in size but grand in his duty, followed with the solemnity of a knight. Our worlds, once orbiting apart, spun into a celestial collision. My pastor from Tampa, whose words had often steered my course, joined us, and my aunt from Delaware, who had shaped my foundation with her matriarchal warmth, graced us with her presence. It was as if the stars themselves had aligned to unite our disparate galaxies. Psalmists lent their voices to our tale, weaving melodies that soared to the heavens, while prophetic declarations etched our story into the annals of time. And then, amidst the scripted vows and rehearsed smiles, spontaneity bloomed. Praise, unfettered and raw, swept through the congregation like a holy gale.

In the eye of this sacred storm, Tony and I found ourselves dancing—our movements less a dance and more a testament of faith. There, in the train of my gown that trailed behind me like the wake of a ship destined for new worlds, we danced for the One who had orchestrated our every step. Our mothers, beacons of strength and grace, watched as their joy became our rhythm. The people all around us were more than guests; they were witnesses to a divine tapestry being woven with threads of our separate pasts. This day was not solely for us but also a testament to a patient God and to a love that had waited. Our years—marked not by the milestones of conventional paths but by the quiet growth of solitary journeys—now converged. We stood, a couple untethered by the expectations of youth, unburdened by paths not taken. Our hands were empty of others to hold, yet full now as they clasped each other. We faced our congregation, our voices rising as we took the sacred vows. The words of Ruth to Naomi were our pledge—a vow that tethered not just two hearts, but two families, two legacies. "Your people shall be my people, and your God shall be my God." Where we would journey, we would journey together; our lodges fused by this sacred covenant. In the echoes of "Amen," we stepped forth, no longer two but one, our union an emblem of a love both ancient and ever new. It was the greatest day of my life! And so, the chapter closed on our solitary days, and the page turned to reveal the dawn of our shared forever.

At the heart of my journey, there lies a truth, sometimes comforting, at other times challenging: the art of waiting is not just about biding time but about being molded by the Master's hands. The local church often echoed the sentiment of waiting, a chorus familiar yet wearisome. "Wait on the Lord," they'd say, a refrain that, despite its repetition, holds a depth of wisdom only appreciated through the lens of maturity. Waiting, I've learned, is not a pause but a process—a prerequisite for every mountain to be climbed, every season to be endured, and every level of growth to be achieved. It's the sacred space between "what is" and "what will be," where faith is both tested and fortified. Philippians 1:6 became my anchor amidst the tempest of uncertainty. "Be confident of this," it declares, "He who began a good work in you will carry it on to completion until the day of Christ Jesus." This promise became a beacon of hope, illuminating the truth that the God who starts a journey in us is faithful to finish it. It reassured me that every dream planted within my heart was not a mere whim but a divine seed destined to grow and flourish. Yet, embracing this truth required a pivotal shift from observing others' journeys to focusing on my own, recognizing that my timeline was uniquely orchestrated by God. The comparison trap, a snare all too easy to fall into, had to be dismantled, brick by brick, with the realization that my story was being penned by the ultimate Author, one who knew the end from the beginning. Psalms 27:14 further encouraged me to "wait on the Lord; be strong, and let your heart take courage; wait for the Lord." Waiting, especially in moments of despair and desolation, can feel like an eternity. Yet, in choosing to be encouraged during the wait, I found strength not just to endure but to thrive. I reminded myself of my worth, my potential, and the divine beauty within me, regardless of my relationship status. "I'm still here," I'd proclaim to my reflection, a declaration of resilience and hope. As the narrative unfolded, and I stepped into the realm of companionship, the values of integrity and living a testimony through actions became paramount. Our lives are a living epistle read by those around us, mattered far more than words could ever convey. It was essential not only to speak of faith but also to embody it, ensuring that our lives echoed the truths we professed. The journey to the altar, then, was not just about the fulfillment of a longing heart but about the testament of a faith journey. It was about reaching a milestone, not just in the context of marital bliss but in the realm of spiritual maturity and divine timing. The night I said "I do" was a culmination of years of waiting, a testament to the faithfulness of God who keeps His promises. In reflection, the scripture from Jude 1:24-25 resonates with profound significance: "Now unto him who is able to keep you from stumbling and to present you blameless before the presence of his glory with great joy..." This verse encapsulates the essence of our journey—God's ability to keep us, to guide us, and to bring us to His appointed time and place with joy unspeakable.

To those walking the path of singleness, my message is one of hope and encouragement. Be confident in the work God is doing in you (Philippians 1:6), embrace the process of waiting with courage (Psalms 27:14), and know that if you desire to be kept, He is more than able to keep you (Jude 1:24-25). My journey is a testament to the faithfulness of God—a narrative of waiting, woven with divine threads, that leads to a tapestry of fulfilled promises and a life lived as a testimony to His glory.

CHAPTER 2

And the Two Shall Become One

When we stood before God and said, "the two shall become one," I did not understand how literal those words would become.

Tony and I did more than share a life—we shared breath, rhythm, and purpose. Between ministry meetings, bedtime prayers, late-night talks, and silent glances across crowded rooms, our souls intertwined so deeply that I no longer recognized where he ended, and I began.

We were not perfect. But we were aligned.

He was strength wrapped in gentleness and vision anchored in faith.

And I was fire, voice, and movement.

Together, we were balanced, a force against darkness.

I entered the marriage whole. I prayed for that. I asked God to heal me before He joined me. I did not want to love from a place of lack. I wanted to love from overflow. And when Tony came into my life, he did not complete me — he confirmed me.

Our wedding day was sacred. When we lit one candle from two flames, it wasn't symbolic poetry. It was a prophecy. We were declaring that from that day forward, there would be no "mine" and "yours." There would only be "ours."

Our dreams merged.

Our ministries merged.

Our families merged.

Even our bodies, prayers, and plans—merged.

We built a life that felt secure. A home full of laughter. A church full of vision. A daughter who carried both of us in her smile. We led together. We fought battles together. We dreamed about the future as if it were guaranteed.

And then, suddenly, one phone call shattered everything.

Life, the Bible says, is like a vapor. I had preached that scripture. I had stood beside grieving families and quoted it with conviction. But when death invaded my house, theology felt hollow in my hands.

Because when you become one with someone, their death doesn't feel like a loss. It feels like an amputation.

It felt like something inside me had been ripped away without anesthesia. The air in my lungs felt thinner. The house felt unfamiliar. Silence became loud. The bed became cruel.

The two had become one.

And now I was forced to live as half of something that was never meant to be divided. People would say, "He's in a better place."

But better for him did not feel better for me.

I was angry.

My anger wasn't at life. It was at God.

Yes — at God.

I trusted Him. I had preached His sovereignty. I had surrendered to His will before. But this? This felt personal. I remember thinking, *Lord, You could have chosen anyone. Why him? Why now?*

Grief stripped me of polished language. My prayers became raw.

"God, this hurts."

"I don't understand you."

"I don't agree with you."

Still, I never walked away.

Because somewhere beneath the anger was a deeper truth that letting go was never an option, as I knew that life without God is a life that would fall completely apart.

I thought about the day we lost our twin baby. I remembered how Tony held me together when I could not hold myself together. He reminded me that we still had life to nurture. We still had love to give. Even in his own grief, he steadied me.

Now, without him, I had to steady myself.

The transition from "we" to "me" was violent: running a home, raising our daughter, leading a church—doing it all alone. Each morning, I faced a reality I did not choose.

Grief became physical. It lived in my chest. It sat in my throat. Some days, I could not get out of bed. Other days, I functioned, but I was hollow. Anger. Sadness. Numbness. They rotated through me like an uninvited cycle.

And then there was the question that haunted me:

Who am I now?

Because when two become one, identity shifts. Decisions shift. Everything shifts. When one is suddenly gone, you not only miss them—you lose a sense of who you were with them. Suddenly, I had to figure out who I was without Tony, apart from our shared identity, and rediscover myself as an individual again.

But here is what grief slowly began to reveal:

I was whole before him.

And I am still whole after him.

Not untouched. Not unscarred. But whole.

Wholeness after loss does not mean you don't ache. It means you discover that your foundation was never another human being — it was God.

Slowly, gratitude began to push back against my anger. Nine years. We had nine beautiful, powerful years. Many people never experience that kind of love. I did. And that is a gift no grave can take.

Tony left a legacy.

He left an impact.

He left a daughter who carries his smile and gentleness.

He left strength in me that I did not know I possessed.

There were days I wanted to stay in grief — because staying there felt like staying close to him. If I healed, did that mean I was moving on? If I smiled again, was I betraying what we had?

God had to teach me that healing is not betrayal.

Grief is love with nowhere to go. And eventually, you must allow that love to turn into strength.

I learned that you can sit in sorrow — but you cannot build your life there. Like David, I had to rise. Wash my face. Worship again. Lead again. Breathe again.

Not because it didn't hurt.

But because the purpose was still calling my name.

The two did become one.

And even though death separated our bodies, it did not erase what God joined. Our covenant did not dissolve at the grave. Our impact did not stop at his last breath.

I am still here.

Still called.

Still chosen.

Still carrying purpose.

And somehow — even in the breaking — God is still faithful.

Reflective Prayer

Father God,

I come to You without polished words.

You saw the vows. You witnessed the covenant. You joined us together. And when death separated us, it felt like You allowed something sacred to be torn apart.

I won't pretend it didn't hurt. It did. It still does.

You know the nights I cried until my body was exhausted.

You know the anger I tried to hide.

You know the questions I was afraid to say out loud.

And yet, you stayed.

Now Lord, for the one reading this prayer, God help them to know that when they are too weak to pray, You still listen to their tears.

Just as I was too angry to worship, You did not withdraw Your presence.

When I felt half of me had died, You reminded me that my identity was always rooted in You. Teach us how to live forward without feeling like we are leaving love behind. Teach us how to carry memory without being crushed by it.

Restore the light that grief tried to dim.

Strengthen the places that are exposed.

Help us to trust You — not only when we understand You, but when we don't.

Thank you for the gift of love.

And thank You that death does not have the final word.

Make our lives a testimony — not just of surviving grief — but of finding You in it.

In Jesus' name,

Amen.

CHAPTER 3
It's Not the End

Death is not the end. I always say this, but April 2021 tested my belief like never before. It was the best and worst month of my life. It was when I said "I do" to the love of my life, and also the time when I thought it was all over. April 12th marked the end of so many joyful experiences with my beloved. No more would our home echo with his random songs from the late 1800s, no more would the clatter of pots and pans fill the air as he cooked meals filled with love. The laughter he shared with his sister, repeating movie lines over and over as if they'd just heard them for the first time, vanished. All those comforting hugs and kisses that pulled me back from the edge, all his unwavering support whenever I stepped up to the pulpit—he made it clear to everyone that I was his favorite preacher—were gone. The days and months since have been incredibly tough, feeling like I've been grappling with the finality of death alone.

What do I do now? That question haunted me after the funerals, after friends stopped visiting, after the calls stopped, and everyone else seemed to quickly move on. I was left figuring out how to manage a mortgage on a six-bedroom house with no current income, how to raise a three-year-old daughter who lost her doting father too soon, and how to lead a burgeoning church through the trials of a pandemic. Despite having supportive leaders, friends, and family, the decisions were mine to make alone. The weight of these decisions pressed down on me—would I lose our house? Could I be both mother and father to my daughter, provide for her, and still serve my church without losing myself? I felt the burden in my heart and my body, becoming a functioning but deeply depressed pastor, mother, daughter, and friend. I wasn't myself; I was changed. As I tried to piece my life back together, I was scared and angry. I learned that being angry with God was pointless. He's sovereign and isn't swayed by our emotions or tantrums. I didn't always agree with Him—I've said this many times—but He does what He wants, knowing what's best even when we disagree. My anger was also fueled by people whispering, questioning my faith, asking why I seemed different, why I wasn't showing Christ's love as Tony would have wanted. I heard it all, and it only made me angrier because I felt judged and perceived as weak. But I wasn't weak in the way they thought; I was overwhelmed by sudden, profound loss. Talking to other widows helped some; those conversations sometimes offered a glimpse of understanding, depending on their timing. Each widow's journey through grief is their testimony, and while my experience felt incredibly lonely, their stories reminded me that I wasn't entirely alone. So, as insensitivity grew around me, I responded not as I taught others—to remain calm and poised—but with raw, unfiltered emotion, sometimes even on social media, trying to inflict a fraction of the pain I was enduring. These weren't my proudest moments, but they were real, raw, and utterly human.

What do I do now? How long until this pain eases? When will life feel normal again? Every corner of our house screams of Tony's love, leaving me to wonder, should I take down his pictures? Should I try to forget him, change the furniture, rearrange the rooms to escape his memory? Depression and fear weren't just visiting; they were taking up residence in my heart and mind. I was more than sad; I was depressed. More than scared, I was terrified. Fear had clenched its grip around my heart. It's essential to understand that the events leading to the announcement of a death can be traumatic. In my case, it was deeply so. I fully expected Tony to come home after what was supposed to be a routine gallbladder surgery. Why wouldn't I? After all, God had lifted him from his sickbed during a bout with COVID just months earlier. Why would this be any different? The memory of that 6 AM phone call from the doctor replays over and over in my mind, jolting me awake at the same time each day. "Hello, may I speak with Mrs. Tate... this is her... is everything OK?" "No," the doctor replied. It was like being stuck in a relentless nightmare with no escape. Every memory from that day is a sharp stab of pain. Driving past the hospital triggers emotional upheavals I can barely manage. This fear of loss has morphed into a fear of dying. What if I'm next? What would happen to my daughter Moriah? The thought of leaving her alone in the world, without siblings, terrifies me. My fear of death started eating away at me, breaking me down bit by bit. Anxiety took over my daily life; I was scared to drive, terrified of flying, and panicking during every bout of turbulence. Whenever Moriah was out of my sight, I imagined the worst: What if someone took her? For months, she couldn't leave my side. If something happened to me, had I prepared enough for her? Was her name on the life insurance? What about my house? Who would raise her? "I can't die yet, Lord!" I would pray. Every ache in my body became a death sentence in my mind. I started monitoring my blood pressure obsessively and scheduling doctors' appointments for symptoms I once ignored. I even thought something was wrong with my heart, only to be told to lay off the Red Bull because it was causing palpitations.

I had never been a fearful person. I was a risk-taker, always putting my full faith in God. But now, fear had trapped me in a place where I struggled to preach about faith while my heart was overrun by fear. I know the opposite of faith is fear, and fear had consumed me. I couldn't recognize the strong, fearless woman I once was. It was humiliating, a secret burden because I couldn't let anyone know I was constantly looking over my shoulder, expecting more bad news. In my desperation, I even bought a gun, keeping it by my bedside, believing I needed to be armed to protect my household. The fear was overwhelming, turning the quiet of my once lively home into something eerie and suffocating. And yes, you might ask, all this because your husband died? Not exactly—it was more than just his physical death. The spirit of fear had crept in like a thief in the night, exploiting the traumatic way I lost Tony. I couldn't understand why he died, causing me to question everything about myself and my faith. Tony was a good man, devoted to God and dedicated to making people happy and leading them to faith. As a child, the saints often reminded us, "To live is Christ, and to die is gain." But in my fear, I'd forgotten how to live. I was so consumed with staying alive that I didn't realize I was actually harming myself. One late night, returning from a ministry event, I broke down and had a real talk with God through tears. My prayer was simple but profound: "Lord, help." I didn't need to say more; God knew the intent of my heart. I was tired of being fearful, exhausted from pretending to be okay. I knew I needed to fight back spiritually, to tear down every thought that doubted my very existence, and I needed to rebuke the spirit of fear. I had to remind myself, "Tash, Death is not the end".

To My Readers

A Note from my heart on Grief and Grace

As you journey through these pages, filled with my rawest moments and darkest days, I hope you find solace in knowing you are not alone in your grief. Each story, each tear, and each smile I've shared is a testament to the unyielding human spirit that connects us all. Grieving is a deeply personal experience, and there is no right or wrong way to navigate through it. It's messy, it's painful, and it often feels like being lost without a map. Yet, there are some things I've found to be helpful along the way. Here are a few things I've learned, which I hope can serve as guiding stars in your own night skies:

Allow Yourself to Feel: Don't rush your healing. Embrace every emotion—let yourself cry, be angry, and even laugh when memories bring joy. Each feeling is a step towards healing.

Seek Support: Lean on friends, family, or find a community. Sometimes, just sharing your thoughts with someone who listens can lighten your burden. You don't have to walk this path alone.

Remember, Love Never Dies: The physical presence of loved ones may pass, but their spirit, their lessons, and the love they left behind continue to live within us. Cherish the memories, for they are timeless.

Give Yourself Grace: Be kind to yourself. Grief can make you feel like you're not yourself. Remember, it's okay to not be okay. You're doing the best you can with the pain you carry.

Turn to Faith: Whether it's spirituality, nature, art, or another form of solace, find something greater that can provide comfort and perspective during tough times.

Live Fully: In honor of those we've lost, let us strive to live fully. To live is to experience all that life offers, to love fiercely, and to act with kindness. Our time here is precious and fleeting—let's make it count.

Remember, dear readers, grief may reshape us, but it does not define us. We are defined by how we rise after falling, how we love in the face of loss, and how we continue to grow with each passing day. May you find peace on your journey, and remember: you are stronger than you think, and death is definitely not the end.

CHAPTER 4

Survivor's Guilt

"For I know the plans I have for you," saith the Lord.

– Jeremiah 29:11

About three or four months after losing my loved one, I began to feel deep guilt for being the parent still spending time with our daughter. I often apologized out loud to my husband for God's decision to call him home. It didn't seem fair, and I was upset with God.

In times of joy, I suppressed my happiness, believing it betrayed my husband. It felt like I was sentenced to sadness. I was hurting, unsure where to place that pain, so I turned it inward. I convinced myself I didn't deserve comfort, happiness, or love, as a part of me felt guilty for living happily in a world without him.

When we married, we became one. When he passed, it felt like part of me left with him. As our daughter grew, she did and said cute, funny things. In the middle of my smile or laugh, I'd realize Tony wasn't there to see it, and my joy would suddenly fade. Many nights, I shouted in anger, "You're missing it all, Tony!" Minutes later, guilt consumed me, and I'd whisper, "Tony, I'm so sorry."

Survivor's remorse is intense psychological distress, often linked to PTSD or tragedy, and comes from needing to make sense of loss. It shows your heart refuses to forget, reflecting how deeply you loved, how interwoven your lives were, and how their absence reshaped your world.

Survivor's guilt settles quietly in your heart, a shadow that follows you even on sunny days. It's the question that keeps circling: **"Why am I still here? Why did I get to stay?"**

It aches when you find yourself laughing, making new plans, or simply waking up to a life forever changed.

How was this choice made?

I often wondered if Tony asked for this during his hospital stay when he said, "Babe, I'm just tired," or if the decision was made for him. These unanswered questions plagued me for years. Everyone loved my husband—he was kind, strong, and always helping people find Christ. He was social and loved to serve. I shared many of his qualities but differed in other ways.

So I questioned, **Why him?**

Why not this person or that person?

My mind sometimes saw individuals who I thought would be better candidates for eternal rest than the love of my life. Yet the only answer God gave me was simple:

"I am God, and I never make a mistake."

We had dreams of taking the world by storm, but one day everything changed. Should I complete them without him? I wanted to fulfill my life, but feeling happiness seemed like betrayal. It wasn't only sorrow from losing someone—it was the ache of being the one left to pick up the pieces. I was lost and torn for some time.

On one hand, I thanked God for my life, health, and strength. On the other hand, I wrestled with guilt. I was grateful to be alive but burdened by knowing my loved one could no longer experience it. Survival felt both wrong and right. I knew each breath was not accidental, but held by a God orchestrating my life behind the scenes, beyond my understanding.

Yet, amid all these emotional shifts, I could not understand ***why***.

I grieved the future that was meant to be shared, the conversations that wouldn't happen, and the aging side by side that had come to an end. Yet even in this pain, I had a reasonable amount of strength for my faith to gently remind me that death is not the end and that separation is not the final word. I am human, and I hurt just like anyone else. Pain is pain regardless of titles or how long you have had a relationship with God.

Someone once said, "I thought she was stronger than this." Honestly, I did too. Don't overestimate yourself. There may be a raging storm or loss that can knock you down, just like Paul or even Job. Survivor's guilt brings self-sabotage—turning down chances, pulling away, or dimming your own joy because good feelings seem wrong.

You might avoid healing, fearing it's forgetting the one you lost. But self-sabotage shows grief seeking a place to land, not brokenness. Hurting yourself emotionally, mentally, or spiritually doesn't honor your loved one. Shrinking your life won't bring them back, nor does punishing yourself deepen your love.

Survivor's guilt hit every time I saw my daughter. My husband had always wanted to be a father, but was told young that he might never have a child because of a rare cancer. He wasn't expected to live long or prosper. Yet God healed him, granting him a wife and later a child.

So again I asked, ***Why him?***

I had to come to the realization that being chosen to live was not a punishment, nor a betrayal. It meant being entrusted to live for now, carrying out every plan orchestrated with God's help. Enjoying every moment that God gives until He returns or until He calls my name. Life is worth living because God never makes a mistake. He is a God who plans things out.

"For I know the plans I have for you... plans of good and not evil, plans to prosper you..."

Healing is not disloyalty. Moving forward doesn't abandon your loved one's memory. Survival was not your choice—it was God's plan. You don't need to justify it daily. I learned I could honor Tony without punishing myself or apologizing for breathing.

With this new clarity, I found I could love Tony while also allowing my own life to unfold. To readers struggling with survivor's guilt, remember: permitting yourself to live and smile is not betrayal. Taking small steps toward the future—no matter how unfamiliar—reflects a healthy shift in your emotions, not a loss of loyalty. Your survival is a testament to the love that continues through you.

Remember that when the guilt rises, quickly remind yourself that your life was not something you stole. It was something you were given. And you are allowed to keep going, one step at a time. You deserve to take up space in the world, even if you are still learning how to do so. You deserve to heal, even if healing sometimes feels like betrayal. You deserve goodness, even if you are afraid to accept it.

Try to notice the moments when you pull back from joy, when you talk yourself out of hope, when you shut down something tender before it has a chance to grow. Those are not signs that you are unworthy. They are signs that you are hurting. And every time you choose compassion toward yourself instead of punishment, you loosen grief's grip just a little more. Let yourself live gently, without earning it or apologizing for it.

You are allowed to keep going.
You are allowed to heal.
You are allowed to build a life that honors God, yourself, and your loved ones.

Doing this will free you from the torment of survivor's guilt. *(Jeremiah 29:11)*

A Prayer for Those Carrying Survivor's Guilt

Heavenly Father,

You see the hidden places of my heart, even the guilt and questions I struggle to understand. Sometimes I carry the weight of surviving when someone I loved did not. I confess that there are moments when joy feels wrong and moving forward feels like betrayal. But today I ask You for peace.

Help me remember that my life is not a mistake and that every breath I take is a gift from You. Give me the strength to honor the memory of the one I lost by living with purpose, love, and faith. Heal the places in my heart where guilt has tried to take root. Replace my sorrow with hope and my confusion with trust in Your plan. Remind me that you are still writing my story. In Jesus' name, Amen.

Practical Steps for Releasing Survivor's Guilt

Grief can sometimes convince us that living fully is somehow a betrayal of the person we lost. Survivor's guilt whispers lies that our joy must now be limited because someone we loved is no longer here to share it. But healing begins when we acknowledge the pain while also accepting that life is still a gift from God. The following exercises are simple ways to begin releasing the weight of survivor's guilt and learning to live again with purpose and peace.

1. Write a Letter to Your Loved One

Take time to write a letter to the person you lost.

Tell them:

- The things you miss most about them
- The memories that still make you smile
- The things happening in your life now
- The things you wish they could see

You can also express the guilt you may still carry.

Many people find healing when they end the letter with something like:

"I will continue living in a way that honors the love we shared."

This exercise allows the heart to release emotions that were never spoken.

2. Replace the "Why Me?" Question

Survivor's guilt often traps us in one question:

"Why did I survive?"

While this question may never have a full answer, try gently shifting it to a new one:

"How can I honor their life by how I live mine?"

This shift does not erase grief, but it helps transform guilt into purpose.

3. Give Yourself Permission to Experience Joy

Many survivors feel guilty the first time they laugh again or feel happiness.

When this happens, pause and remind yourself:

- Joy does not erase love.
- Happiness does not mean you forgot them.
- Living fully does not dishonor their memory.

Instead of seeing joy as betrayal, begin to see it as **evidence that life is still moving forward with God's grace.**

4. Practice Compassion Toward Yourself

When guilt rises, speak to yourself the way you would comfort a friend.

Instead of saying:

- *"I shouldn't feel happy."*

Try saying:

- *"It's okay to keep living."*

Healing is not forgetting. Healing is learning to carry love and loss at the same time.

Scriptures for Those Struggling with Survivor's Guilt

God's Word reminds us that life is not random and that His plans continue even when we do not understand them. Parents, pastors, or readers may find comfort in meditating on these scriptures during seasons of grief.

Jeremiah 29:11
"For I know the plans I have for you," declares the Lord, "plans to prosper you and not to harm you, plans to give you hope and a future."

Psalm 30:5
"Weeping may endure for a night, but joy comes in the morning."

Isaiah 43:2
"When you pass through the waters, I will be with you."

Romans 8:28
"And we know that all things work together for good to those who love God."

2 Corinthians 1:3–4
"The Father of compassion and the God of all comfort... comforts us in all our troubles."

Psalm 73:26
"My flesh and my heart may fail, but God is the strength of my heart."

CHAPTER 5

Learning to Live Through the Triggers

It was an ordinary morning.

Driving my daughter to school, the day felt normal. The sun was out. For once, I could breathe without the familiar weight on my chest.

Then I saw it.

To my right, a familiar sign: *Hospital — Next Signal.*

I had passed that sign before. But now, it felt less like a sign and more like a doorway.

Before I could gather my thoughts, I was no longer in my car. I was back in that room.

The smell of antiseptic.

The sound of the monitors.

The sight of my beloved husband lying there.

The weight of knowing that place, and of my first goodbye, hit me like a ton of bricks.

My hands tightened around the steering wheel.

My chest felt like it was collapsing inward.

Tears came—violent and uninvited.

And in that moment, I realized something important: **Triggers are a normal part of grief that remind us how deeply we have loved and lost.**

They are the echoes of experiences our hearts are not ready to release.

In my early years of grief, I was easily triggered.

It was hard to hear the name 'Tony'.

It was hard to catch the scent of the cologne he used to wear.

It was hard to hear the songs he sang at church.

Everything was a reminder, a reopening.

I was, in every sense, overwhelmed by trigger*s*.

So, I tried to protect myself—I shrank my world.

I became a hermit in my own home, trying to avoid anything that might stir anger, sadness, or longing. But even in isolation, grief found me. And on top of my own triggers, I had to witness the pain of others being triggered, too.

Seeing their grief... triggered mine.

So, I started positioning my life around avoidance.

I stayed away from couples, or I forced smiles so I wouldn't make them uncomfortable.

I avoided weddings.

I avoided funerals.

Because no matter who stood at the altar or lay in the casket...

I saw him.

One of the clearest moments I remember was my middle sister's wedding day.

My sister's wedding was one of her happiest days, and I wanted to be there for her. We are close.

But something inside me whispered, *"Don't do it."*

Still, I couldn't miss it. This was my sister.

I entered the church, made my way to my seat, clutching my pearls. I smiled, feeling genuinely happy for her.

Then the doors opened.

She began walking down the aisle to the song, *"The One He Kept for Me"* by Maurette Brown Clark.

The same song I walked down the aisle to.

Suddenly, emotion welled up, threatening to overwhelm me.

Overwhelmed, I tried to keep it together as emotion rushed in—tears filled my eyes.

Grief... not right now.

But grief does not wait for convenient moments.

I quickly slipped out of the row, rushed down the side aisle, and made my way to the nearest exit.

I never made it back inside.

I was embarrassed. Not because I wasn't happy for my sister, but because in that moment, I was confronted with how deeply I was still hurting.

It wasn't about her joy.

It was about my loss.

Grief has a powerful memory.

When it's triggered, it can either bring a gentle reminder of something beautiful... or a sharp reminder of something that shattered you. And if we don't learn how to manage those moments, they can pull us under.

A Biblical Moment That Helped Me Breathe Again

One of the most powerful examples of a trigger in Scripture is found in Peter's story.

After Jesus was crucified, Peter carried more than grief—he carried regret. He had denied Jesus three times before the rooster crowed.

Scripture tells us that when the rooster crowed, Peter remembered what Jesus had said—and he wept bitterly.

That sound became tied to heartbreak.

Now imagine living somewhere where roosters crow every morning.

Every sunrise could have been a reminder.

Every sound could have pierced his heart.

That is what a trigger feels like.

But what moves me deeply is what Jesus did next.

After the resurrection—after proving that death was not the end—Jesus met Peter by a charcoal fire.

The only other time Scripture mentions a charcoal fire was the night Peter denied Him.

The setting itself was a trigger.

But Jesus didn't avoid it.

He chose it.

He met Peter there.

He restored him there.

He redeemed him there.

The very place tied to Peter's pain became the place of his restoration.

And that helped me understand something life-changing: Although triggers will come, God can meet us in those painful moments, offering comfort and healing right where we hurt most.

Sometimes, he doesn't remove the trigger right away.

In His wisdom, He meets us there—and teaches us how to breathe again.

What Triggers Reveal About My Heart

Triggers are tied to the moments that marked us forever.

The last conversation.

The hospital room.

The funeral.

The silence that followed.

That morning in my car, I wasn't just seeing a sign.

I was remembering love.

I was remembering presence.

I was remembering the sacred weight of that final season.

For a moment, it felt like I was reliving it.

But I wasn't.

I was carrying it.

And there is a difference.

A trigger is not meant to trap me in the past but can instead become a place where healing begins.

It can become holy ground.

A place where God whispers:

"I was there then. I am here now. And this is still not the end."

What I Do Now When the Waves Return

I don't respond the way I used to.

At first, I panicked, thinking I was going backward and judging myself for crying.

Now, I respond with grace.

1. Pause Instead of Panic

When I pass that sign now, I pause. I breathe.

"This is a memory. I am safe. God is here."

Sometimes I whisper, "Tony, I miss you."

But I don't let my mind go too far back. I remind myself:

I am not in that hospital room.

I am alive.

I am still breathing.

And my loved one is resting in the bosom of our Father.

Remembering love does not mean death has won.

2. Put a name to what you feel

"This hurts because this sign represents that day I had to say goodbye."

Naming it brings clarity.

Unidentified pain feels chaotic.

Named pain feels manageable.

3. Invite God into your Memory

Just like Jesus met Peter by that fire, I invite God into my moments.

"Lord, You were with us in that room. Be with me now."

And in that quiet space, I feel steadied.

And when I invite Him in, I feel that closeness.

4. Let the Feeling Move Through You

I let the tears fall.

Not endlessly.

Not without hope.

Then I wipe my face and keep moving.

Healing doesn't mean I stop feeling.

It means I no longer drown in what I feel.

The Redemption of Triggers

I imagine Peter hearing a rooster crow after being restored.

I don't believe it pierced him the same way anymore.

After grace, that sound didn't just represent failure—it represented forgiveness.

That's what I believe God can do for us.

That hospital sign no longer only reminds me of loss.

It reminds me that although something tragic happened, I don't have to fall apart in that memory.

A sign that once shattered you, can one day be reminded of love more than loss.

An anniversary that once brought dread can become a day of honoring.

A place that once felt unbearable can become sacred ground.

God does not waste our pain.

He redeems it.

And redemption is proof that death does not have the final say.

A Gentle Reminder for You

If something small brought tears to your eyes today... You are not broken.

You are remembering.

If a sound shifted your heart unexpectedly... You are not regressing.

You are human.

Even Peter wept when a sound reminded him of his pain.

But that was not the end of his story.

And this is not the end of yours.

One day, there will be no more triggers—because there will be no more separation.

The same God who defeated the grave will wipe every tear.

The same Savior who restored Peter will complete your healing.

Until then, anchor yourself in this truth: **Triggers will come, but they do not have to derail your emotions or your response. They also do not have the power to destroy you.**

With God, you can walk through every single one of them.

You don't have to do it alone.

He always provides what you need—even in grief.

Closing Prayer

Father,

Thank You that even when memories feel overwhelming, Your promise still stands.

When a song, a sign, a scent, or a date pulls me back, remind me that I am not trapped in that moment—I am carried by Your grace.

Meet me in every trigger.

Turn painful reminders into sacred ground.

Redeem what aches and restore what feels fragile.

Help me hold onto this truth when emotions rise:

It's not the end.

Not for the one I love.

And not for me.

In Jesus' name,

Amen.

CHAPTER 6

Scheduled Sadness

Grief taught my heart how to remember time differently. It was never just about what happened. It was about when it happened. My body began to keep its own calendar, and my soul followed a clock that no one else could see. Without trying, I found myself circling the same days, the same hours, and the same seasons, as if something deep within me whispered, this is the day everything fell apart. I never consciously planned it, but I could feel it as certain dates approached. A heaviness would settle over me without warning. My energy would shift. My thoughts would slow, and I would withdraw without fully understanding why.

It was not weakness.

It was a memory.

Grief lived deeper than my thoughts. It settled in my nervous system, took hold of my emotions, and hid in the quiet places of my heart—those parts that learned to link specific moments in time with pain. Sometimes, grief felt like an unspoken appointment. Though I never wrote it down, my body showed up faithfully every time.

Birthdays, anniversaries, and the dates connected to his death and funeral all carried a weight of their own. On those days, I felt fragile. Tears came more easily. Joy felt distant. It was as if part of me returned to stand at the doorway of what I had lost, honoring it while also feeling trapped in memories I could not escape. For the first few years, my grief even followed me into my sleep. Every Monday at 6 a.m., I would wake up in a cold sweat, my heart racing as if I were still waiting for the doctor's phone call that had changed my life.

My body remembered what my mind tried to move beyond. Sleep became interrupted. My days grew heavier. I was functioning but exhausted from reliving moments I could not change. Sometimes, I would be laughing, fully present, when a sudden wave of heaviness came over me. It seemed to come from nowhere. I would stop and ask myself, What is this? Why do I feel this way?

Eventually, I realized it was not random. It was my spirit remembering. It was tied to a date, a moment, an experience that had left a permanent imprint on my heart. The days that once held celebrations became the days I began to dread. Birthdays, anniversaries, holidays, and ordinary moments we once shared all carried two realities at once. They reminded me of the joy we lived and the absence I now carry.

My heart remembered everything—both consciously and unconsciously—and those memories could interrupt my peace without permission. There was also a strange sense of obligation attached to those days. It was as if I was supposed to be sad, as if grief was the only appropriate response. I would schedule PTO days without always having to admit why. I would leave the day open, already believing I would not have the strength to carry anything else.

Without realizing it, I had begun scheduling my sadness. As those dates approached, I would grow emotionally distant. I would become more reflective. I would allow myself to feel everything I had held together for the rest of the year. I could function, smile, serve, and survive on other days, but when those days came, my heart told the truth. Loss had changed me. Love had changed me. And part of me believed that honoring him meant allowing myself to fall apart.

Sometimes it even felt wrong to smile. Peace felt unfamiliar, almost disloyal. It was as if my grief was the last thread connecting me to him. So I made space for sadness. I expected it. I surrendered to it before the day even arrived. But, over time, I began asking myself difficult questions.

How do I know I will be sad on that day?

Who said I have to suffer when the sun rises on that date?

When did grief become the authority over my life?

I began to realize that scheduling my sadness was giving grief more power than it deserved. My grief was real, but it was not my master. It did not get to dictate my peace. It did not get to decide whether I would live or merely exist. If sadness came, I allowed it. But I stopped assuming it had to come. I also realized something deeper in my faith. By deciding in advance that my day would be filled with sorrow, I left no room for God to meet me there in a different way. I was not allowing space for His comfort, His peace, or His presence. I began to understand that those days did not only belong to trauma. They also belonged to God.

God could still bring healing to places that once held pain. My grief existed because love existed first. The pain was evidence that something meaningful had lived in my life. Healing did not erase those dates; it gave me power to respond to them differently. I became intentional. Instead of letting those days hold only sorrow, I gave them new meaning.

I prayed and gave my day to God. I asked Him to free me from fear, oppression, and old emotional traps. I asked for peace in my sleep and strength in my waking. I stopped believing I would always suffer. I replaced scheduling sadness with ***scheduling honor***.

Sometimes I would release balloons into the sky. Sometimes I invite friends and family to sit with me in love and remembrance. Other times, I planned outings that reminded me I was still alive. I gave myself permission to create new experiences on days that once held great sorrow. Some days were easier than others. Sometimes I started the day strong and ended in tears. Other times, I woke up heavy and ended the day with unexpected peace.

I kept being intentional. I kept choosing life even when grief tried to pull me backward. I learned that creating new memories did not mean I was forgetting him. It meant I was reclaiming myself. Over time, those days loosened their grip on me. They no longer controlled me the way they once had. I still remembered, but I was no longer consumed. I was no longer just surviving those dates. I was living through them with the strength I did not know I had. What once felt like days of only sorrow became days of reflection, honor, and even gratitude. Gratitude for the love we shared. Gratitude for the strength God placed within me. Grateful that I was still here. One day, I realized something had changed. The sadness still visited, but it no longer came alone.

Peace was there too.

Strength was there.

Healing was there.

And so was I. ***Still standing.***

A Prayer for Difficult Dates

Heavenly Father,

Today is one of those days that carries memories my heart cannot ignore. The calendar may mark it as just another date, but for me, it holds moments, emotions, and reminders of a life that changed forever.

You know the weight that certain days carry. You see the memories that rise without warning, the emotions that return when I least expect them, and the quiet moments when my heart feels tender again.

Lord, I bring this day to You.

I ask you to meet me in every memory that surfaces. When sadness appears, give me comfort. When tears fall, remind me that You are close to the brokenhearted. When my mind drifts back to painful moments, gently bring peace to my spirit.

Help me remember that grief exists because love existed first. Thank you for the memories I was able to share with the one I lost. Thank you for the time, the laughter, the lessons, and the love that will always remain a part of my life.

On days like this, remind me that I am not alone. You are with me in the quiet moments, in the memories, and in the healing that is still unfolding.

Give me the strength to honor the past without being trapped by it. Help me create space for both remembrance and peace.

Fill this day with Your presence.

Where grief once held all the space, allow healing to grow. Where sadness visits, let Your comfort sit beside it. And where my heart feels fragile, remind me that Your grace is still carrying me forward.

Thank You for the love that once filled my life, and for the strength You continue to give me each day.

In Jesus' name,

Amen.

CHAPTER 7

Even the Smallest Hearts Mourn

Dealing with grief as an adult is one thing, however watching my young child grieve brought a new pain. Like many parents, I want to protect my child at all costs. I feel responsible for creating a carefree life—a life free from heartache if possible. Yet as much as I tried to shield my daughter, some things are beyond my control.

The death of a loved one is one kind of pain. But losing the first people you meet in life is something parents simply cannot prevent.

On April 12th, I stand here. First, I struggle to accept the news myself. Now, I must explain to my three-year-old daughter that her "*DA DA*" will not come home from the hospital. She will never again feel his big hugs, hear his soothing voice, or ride with him to Walmart to pick her favorite toys.

Immediately, memories returned of my father being absent as a child. He was alive, but chose to stay away because of an ongoing feud with my mother. I didn't want to participate in things like the daddy-daughter dance because he was gone. I often wished

I had more time with him when I was growing up. I would see him play with my baby brother and wish I could have felt that same bond as the firstborn.

My heart broke, assuming my daughter would feel the same loneliness I knew from my own absent father. Although my dad and I rebuilt our relationship by high school, I knew MJ would never have that chance.

“Don't worry, Tasha. Moriah will be just fine.”

“Hey, she’s just three years old. She won't even remember much anyway.”

“Children are resilient at her age; they usually bounce back quickly.”

“Don't you take her to that funeral, she's too young.”

These are just a few statements offered to me during my time of despair. Each meant to help me figure out how to deliver this blow.

How do I explain death to a baby?

I mean, he left the house because of a tummy ache and never returned. This was hard to deal with, let alone explain. I remember calling my Bishop, Bishop Eric D. Garnes, one evening. I was sobbing as I told him my fear of how to tell my three-year-old. His counsel that day was clear.

“Pastor Tate, tell her the truth!”

Huh? What do you mean by truth?

When I was a little girl, they told me that our loved ones were up in heaven with Jesus. They told me that God had need of our loved ones in heaven.

He reiterated to me again, "Pastor Tate, tell her the truth."

He then said it is important to tell her the truth. He explained that if you say her father is in the sky with Jesus, she may first become angry with God for taking him, or later resent her father for choosing to leave to be with Jesus. Recognizing this, he advised telling her the truth in a way a three-year-old can understand. When I spoke to my daughter that night, I told her the truth as simply as I could. At first, she would forget and ask again and again, but each time, I patiently told her the truth, sharing a little more as she grew and her questions deepened.

Telling the truth is key.

Parents often withhold information from children to protect them, but this can sometimes add to trauma. Now, at eight, she is fully aware that if she lives a life pleasing to God, she shall see Tony again. As I experienced my own grief, I saw early on that Moriah was going through the same, though her response was different.

Parents often forget that children grieve too—not from lack of care, but because their own grief overwhelms and drains their emotional energy. Everyone grieves differently. Adults grasp loss as permanent. Children, especially young ones like Moriah Joi', show grief in many ways—crying one moment, playing the next. This can make it seem children are fine, but it's just their way of processing emotions in small doses.

After losing my spouse, I panicked and went into survival mode. I managed daily responsibilities, sometimes eating, sometimes not. I tried to handle finances, funeral arrangements, and the needs of other family and church members. The emotional weight made it hard to make sense of the loss, and I sometimes missed the subtle ways Moriah expressed her pain. Grieving children, like adults, can have behavioral changes or physical symptoms—such as headaches or stomachaches. Sometimes, children need more attention because most of it is directed toward the parent or adult.

Moriah would often cry over the loss of her daddy. When she was around four, I noticed she could be fine one moment, but if she saw me upset, she felt she had to be upset too. I didn't notice it right away. But as I had my breakdowns, I saw that she would start to break down too—always watching me. When I was better, so was she. The Holy Spirit brought this to my attention. I began to talk to her more about her feelings. I explained that Mommy has her feelings, and Moriah has hers. If you are happy, you don't have to be sad if Mommy is sad. And I don't have to be sad if Moriah is sad. It was a teachable moment amid our grief.

When parents pause to notice these signs and create space for honest conversation, children feel seen—and that helps them heal. Shared grief, even in small ways, becomes a bridge keeping families connected rather than isolated. Knowing many parents in my situation would never have allowed their children to attend a funeral—let alone two—so young, I did not want to take away the chance for Moriah to see her father's body one last time. It was a decision I made for my daughter, and I am still proud of it today. Moriah is now a thriving, beautiful eight-year-old, encouraged to process and discuss her feelings.

She knows it's okay to miss her daddy. She knows she can feel pain and happiness at any moment. As parents or adults, when we pause to see that children mourn too and respond with love and patience, healing begins. Children may hold on tighter at bedtime. They might not have words to explain, but their hearts know loss as deeply as ours. When we meet their grief with love and patience, something powerful happens. It builds trust and deepens the bonds of love.

To the Parents or Guardians of Grieving Little Ones

In your own heartbreak, remember there are little hearts beside you. They are watching, listening, and feeling too. Their grief may not sound like yours. It may show in many forms. But their pain is real. Their hearts are learning how to carry sorrow and still keep faith by watching you.

It's okay for them to see your tears. Let them know sadness and strength can live in the same soul. When they see you lean on God in weakness, they learn grief does not mean a lack of faith. Do not rush your healing, or theirs.

Grief has no finish line.

As you walk through this together, remember God's presence remains in pain. He is near the brokenhearted. Grieve, and let God's Spirit comfort you as you comfort them. You are not alone. God's grace carries you.

A Prayer for Children Who Are Missing Someone They Love

Dear God,

Sometimes our hearts feel sad because we miss someone we love very much.

Thank you for loving us and staying close when we feel lonely or hurt.

Help us remember the good memories we shared and fill our hearts with peace.

Remind us that you are always with us and that your love never leaves us.

In Jesus' name, Amen.

Grief can be confusing for children because they often lack words to explain their feelings. Sometimes their sadness appears as questions, behavior changes, or silence. Creating safe, gentle spaces for children to share their emotions can help them process loss in a healthy way.

Below are a few simple exercises parents and caregivers can use to help children move through grief with love, patience, and faith.

1. The Memory Drawing Exercise

Invite your child to draw a picture of their loved one or a happy memory they shared together.

You can ask simple questions such as:

- What is your favorite memory with them?
- What made you smile when you were with them?
- What would you want them to know today?

For younger children, drawing is often easier than talking. Their artwork can be a special way to remember the person they lost. Consider making a "Memory Box" where drawings, photos, or small keepsakes can be placed to honor that loved one.

2. Feelings Check-In

Children may not always know how to explain their emotions. Helping them name their feelings can be powerful.

You can ask questions like:

- Are you feeling sad today?
- Do you feel angry?
- Do you miss Daddy/Mommy/Grandma today?

You can also use a simple feelings scale:

- Happy
- Okay
- Sad
- Mad

Draw pictures or print images of emojis. Let them point to the face that best represents how they feel. This helps children learn that all emotions are allowed and safe to share.

3. Talking to Heaven

For families who practice faith, this can be a comforting exercise.

Invite your child to say a prayer or speak a message to their loved one.

You might say something like:

"If you could say something to Daddy right now, what would you want him to know?"

Children often find comfort in knowing that love continues even when someone is no longer physically present.

This can also become part of bedtime prayer.

4. The Hug and Hold Moment

Grief can make children feel uncertain or unsafe. Sometimes what they need most is physical reassurance. Create a daily moment where you:

- Hug your child
- Sit together quietly
- Let them talk if they want

You might say:

"It's okay to miss Daddy. Mommy misses him, too."

Shared comfort helps children understand that they are not grieving alone.

5. The "Remembering Day" Tradition

Occasionally, choose a special day to remember the loved one together.

You might:

- Look at pictures
- Share funny stories
- Visit a place they loved
- Say a prayer together.

This teaches children that remembering someone we love is a healthy part of healing, not something to avoid.

A Final Encouragement for Parents

Helping a child grieve does not mean you have to have all the answers. What children need most is honesty, patience, and reassurance that they are safe and loved. Your presence, your willingness to listen, and your faith will guide them more than perfect words ever could.

As Psalm 34:18 reminds us:

"The Lord is close to the brokenhearted and saves those who are crushed in spirit."

Even the smallest hearts mourn, but with love, truth, and God's comfort, they can also heal. Reading these scriptures together can help remind children that even when someone they love is no longer here, God is always near. Parents and caregivers can read these verses with their children during quiet moments, bedtime, or prayer time.

Matthew 5:4
"Blessed are those who mourn, for they will be comforted."

Psalm 147:3
"He heals the brokenhearted and binds up their wounds."

John 14:27
"Peace I leave with you; my peace I give you... Do not let your hearts be troubled and do not be afraid."

Isaiah 41:10
"Do not fear, for I am with you... I will strengthen you and help you."

Revelation 21:4
"He will wipe every tear from their eyes. There will be no more death or mourning or crying or pain."

Psalm 23:4
"Even though I walk through the darkest valley, I will fear no evil, for you are with me."

Romans 8:38–39
"Nothing can separate us from the love of God."

CHAPTER 8

A Widow's Walk

There was a dizzying disorientation in shifting from married to single. It wasn't by choice, nor by drifting apart, nor by divorce, but by death. I had not prepared for this transition. There were no lessons, no rituals. No words felt adequate. It simply overtook me.

One day, I was living inside the gentle pulse of "we," and the next, the world handed me the word "single," as if nothing meaningful had ended in between. But something sacred was lost. Marriage wove itself into everything. It shaped how I woke, planned my day, prayed, and pictured the future. It changed my speech, my thinking, and the way I moved through a room.

Especially in the church, I grew up hearing, "The two shall become one." Not just a poetic phrase, but a promise. A merging. A holy covenant. Over time, the shift happened so naturally that I hardly noticed it. "I" became "we." "Mine" became "ours." Even the smallest decisions were shared out loud. Life became shared weight and shared refuge. I didn't just live beside him. I lived intertwined.

When death arrived, it didn't just take a person—it shattered a whole way of being. I was expected to untangle a life never meant to exist alone again. Then came the word: single. It sounded clinical, detached, almost dismissive. "Single" implied availability, independence, and a blank slate. But nothing about me was blank.

My heart was not empty. It was full.

Full of memory.

Full of covenant.

Full of late-night conversations and inside jokes and prayers whispered while holding hands in the dark.

Love did not evaporate just because breathing stopped. It took me some time to understand something important: I wasn't unmarried. I was widowed, and there is a difference.

Unmarried implies absence. Widowhood proves love existed. Widowhood aches uniquely—quiet and unpredictable. It arrives in mundane moments without warning: signing paperwork alone, making decisions solo, entering couples' rooms, and suddenly sensing a missing chair at my table. I remember the first time I faced an important form and saw the question:

Married, single, divorced, or widowed?

That single question caused pain. I had to accept a title I never asked for. Years later, the wound still stings. It feels like reaching for a hand that isn't there, turning to share a thought, and finding only silence. Often, grief doesn't cry aloud—sometimes, it just sits beside you and breathes.

There is also a strange grief in how other couples begin to see you. Some don't know what to say. Others treat you like fragile glass. But grief does not run on calendars. Love does not expire with time. Just because I wear this title does not mean I stopped being a wife overnight. It took me time to learn to shift my mind and understand that I was now an individual again.

Spiritually, the shift shook me in ways I didn't expect. Not because I stopped believing, but because I trusted God with my marriage. We prayed together. We built our home under His covering. I thanked Him for the gift of companionship.

And now I was walking forward alone—still faithful, still trusting, but undeniably changed.

As a widow, some scriptures landed differently, and some sermons stung. Messages about companionship—once comforting—now felt like salt in an invisible wound. I found myself wrestling with God. My struggle was not with disbelief, but with heartbreak.

"Lord, we served You together. Why am I walking this road alone?"

And yet, even in this space, God was near. Scripture reminds us that He is "a father to the fatherless, a defender of widows" (Psalm 68:5).

Defender, not observer. Not a distant comforter. Defender.

God had to help me rebuild my identity all over again.

Isaiah 54:5 says, "For your Maker is your husband, the Lord Almighty is His name."

This scripture didn't replace or erase my love; it sustained me when loneliness was unbearable. I felt His presence in tearful prayers, early morning stillness, and the strength to get out of bed. Learning to live single again was hard. It wasn't about becoming strong, but honest.

Honest about my grief.

Honest about my anger.

Honest about my embarrassment.

There were moments I didn't expect to feel embarrassed, but I was. Not ashamed of loving him. Not ashamed of our story. But embarrassed by the title that followed me into rooms like an invisible label across my chest.

Widow.

It felt like everyone could see it before I spoke. Amid rooms full of couples laughing and holding hands, I became aware of my empty chair, my single plate, and my quiet walk to the car. I hated feeling so exposed. I didn't just feel different.

I felt marked. Conversations shifted when people asked, "So, are you married?" Every time, there was a pause before I answered—heavier than it should be. Saying "I'm widowed" felt like dropping something fragile and watching people scramble to respond. Faces softened. Voices fell. Heads tilted. Pity seeped in. In those moments, I didn't feel strong, brave, or faithful. I felt small.

Sometimes I wished I could blend in again—just for a night, just for one gathering—without being the reminder that love can end in loss. I would sit in church pews or at dinner tables and feel like I didn't fit the picture anymore. Like everyone else had a matching set, and I was the single piece left over. It was strange how quickly I could go from feeling secure in who I was to feeling self-conscious about simply existing.

I found myself overexplaining, oversmiling, trying to make others comfortable with my reality—as if my pain needed to be managed for them. That was exhausting. Widowhood isn't carried only in your heart; sometimes it feels like it's on your skin. Yet, God began to correct my thoughts—reminding me I wasn't an interruption, or a tragic story walking in late. I wasn't less than or left behind.

There was evidence that love had been real and sacred. If anything, widowhood did not make me smaller—it made me a living testimony of how God can keep a woman or man who has loved and lost through death. Today, I don't walk in shame. What I once felt embarrassed about, God began to show me was holy.

My story wasn't something to hide. It was something He was still holding. So even when I walk into rooms alone now, I remind myself:

I am not incomplete.

I am not forgotten.

I am not "just" a widow.

I am a woman who was loved deeply, who is still being carried by God. Learning that being single through loss didn't mean I was broken—it meant I had loved fully—was important. Love leaves an imprint, and God honors my honesty, not the speed of my recovery.

I gave myself permission to go slow; healing became my virtue. Grief changed my capacity. What once felt easy now took courage. I chose safe people—those who honored my husband's memory, didn't rush me, and let tears fall without fixing them. With them, I didn't have to perform strength.

I just got to be. I learned to speak my limits out loud.

"Today is hard."

"I may leave early."

"I'm grateful to be here, even if I'm quiet."

Honesty built bridges for me. Pretending only built walls. I began to understand that grief and gratitude can coexist. I could celebrate other couples' love and still mourn my own. I could laugh and ache in the same breath. Sometimes faith looked like showing up trembling. Sometimes it looked like staying five minutes longer than the last time. Sometimes it looked like whispering, "Help me, Lord," under my breath. And that happened often.

As I healed, I learned God wasn't asking me to replace what I lost. He was rebuilding me—not into who I was, but into someone greater. Someone who carries compassion, understands sorrow, and still chooses hope. Reconnection came in layers—by grace, not force. One day, I found myself in a room full of couples, not feeling invisible, forgotten, or incomplete—but held and known. Widowhood is not the end of my story; it is evidence that I loved well. A love like that never disappears; it changes shape. And in His faithfulness, God keeps walking with me—one day, one minute, one breath, one prayer, one step at a time.

Rebuilding Life After Loss

Rebuilding identity after the loss of a spouse is slow and rarely neat. It unfolds quietly, often unexpectedly. Widowhood reshapes how a person sees themselves and how they move through the world. Life, once structured and shared, becomes unfamiliar terrain. Simple decisions, once discussed together, now fall quietly to one person. Even the most ordinary moments change when the one who shared them is gone.

Yet rebuilding identity is not about erasing the love that once existed. It is about learning how to carry that love in a new way. The memories, laughter, prayers, and experiences shared within a marriage do not disappear simply because life has changed. Instead, those memories become part of the foundation that helps shape the person you are becoming. A widow does not begin again as an empty slate. She carries a story written in love, sacrifice, companionship, and covenant. That story remains a part of who she is, even as God gently leads her into a new chapter.

For many widows, one of the hardest parts of healing is allowing themselves the freedom to grow again. Growth can feel uncomfortable, even disloyal at times. There may be moments when laughter returns and a small voice inside wonders if joy is allowed. There may be days when life begins to feel lighter, and with that lightness comes a strange sense of guilt. But healing does not mean forgetting. Moving forward does not mean leaving love behind. Instead, it means allowing that love to continue shaping who you are while also making room for the life that still remains ahead.

Widowhood often reveals strengths that were never fully recognized before. The same person who once leaned on a partner for companionship and support begins to discover new layers of resilience, courage, and faith. The road may feel lonely at times, but it also becomes a place where God's presence often feels closer than ever before. In the quiet moments of prayer, in the stillness of early mornings, and in the unexpected strength to face another day, many widows begin to recognize that God is walking beside them in ways they had never fully understood before.

There is also beauty in the way compassion begins to grow through grief. Those who have loved deeply and lost deeply often develop a tenderness toward others who are hurting. Pain has a way of opening the heart to empathy and understanding. Experiences that once felt isolating slowly become part of a testimony that can bring comfort to others walking similar paths. In this way, the pain of loss does not remain meaningless. God can use it to cultivate wisdom, gentleness, and compassion that blesses the lives of others.

It is important for widows to remember that healing is not measured by how quickly life returns to normal. In truth, life rarely returns to what it once was. Instead, healing is the slow process of learning how to live fully again while honoring the love that shaped the past. Some days will feel strong and hopeful. Other days may still carry waves of grief. Both experiences can exist within the same journey.

The goal is not to rush forward, but to continue walking faithfully one step at a time.

As time moves forward, many widows discover that their identity is not defined by the loss they experienced, but by the love they shared and the strength that carried them through. Widowhood may become a chapter of their story, but it is not the final sentence. Life continues to unfold, often in ways that cannot yet be seen. And in the middle of that unfolding, God continues to write.

From my heart to the heart of widows everywhere:

If you are reading these words as someone who has lost a spouse, I want you to know first and foremost that you are not alone. Widowhood can feel like walking through a world that suddenly speaks a language you never asked to learn. The life you once knew changed in ways that no one could have prepared you for, and sometimes it may feel as though everyone around you has continued moving forward while you are still learning how to breathe in a space that feels unfamiliar. There will be days when the silence feels louder than any noise. There will be moments when memories arrive unexpectedly, bringing both warmth and pain. You may find yourself reaching for the person who once stood beside you, only to be reminded again that their presence has changed. Those moments can feel incredibly heavy, and it is important to know that feeling that weight does not make you weak. It simply means that you loved deeply.

Grief after losing a spouse is not something that can be measured or rushed. Some days you may feel strong and steady, able to carry the memories with quiet gratitude. Other days may feel fragile, when even the smallest reminder can bring tears to the surface. Both of these experiences are part of the same journey. Healing does not mean that the love you shared fades away. In many ways, that love becomes part of the strength that continues to carry you forward. You may also discover that widowhood changes the way you see yourself. The roles that once defined your daily life may now feel uncertain. The identity of "wife" or "husband" that once shaped your routines and conversations may feel difficult to let go of. This transition can be confusing, and at times it may even feel like a part of your identity has been taken with the loss. But over time, many widows begin to discover that their story did not end with that chapter. Instead, a new chapter unfolds—one that carries both the love that was and the life that still remains.

There may also be moments when you question whether it is acceptable to experience joy again. Laughter may return quietly, and when it does, it may surprise you. You might wonder if allowing yourself to feel happiness somehow dishonors the person you lost. But the truth is that love does not demand that we live in sorrow forever. The love you shared was never meant to trap you in grief. Instead, it can become part of the courage that keeps you living fully. God understands the path you are walking. The Scriptures remind us that He is a defender of widows and one who stays close to the brokenhearted. Even when you cannot see clearly what lies ahead, God continues to walk beside you. He sees the strength it takes to get out of bed on difficult mornings. He hears the prayers whispered in quiet moments. He understands the tears that come without warning. And through it all, His presence remains steady.

As time moves forward, you may find that your heart begins to heal in ways you never expected. The sharp edges of grief may soften, and memories that once brought only pain may begin to carry warmth again. You may discover new parts of yourself—strength you did not know you had, compassion for others who are hurting, and a deeper understanding of how precious life truly is. None of this means that you have forgotten your spouse. It simply means that your love has found a new way to live within you.

So if today feels heavy, take it one moment at a time. You do not have to have all the answers for tomorrow. You only need strength for today. Allow yourself grace as you navigate this journey. Surround yourself with people who honor your story and respect your healing process. And most importantly, remember that your life still carries purpose. Widowhood may have changed the path you expected to walk, but it has not erased the value of your life or the beauty of the story God is still writing.

Your love was real.

Your grief is valid.

Your healing is possible.

And even now, step by step, God is still walking beside you.

CHAPTER 9

A Journey to Love After Loss

Losing a spouse is a kind of heartbreak that reshapes life itself. For years, I had become accustomed to a certain way of living, with a consistent routine and a sense of security about my future. The love Tony and I shared didn't fade; it remained at the forefront of my heart. Forgetting wasn't the problem.

Silence and emptiness now fill my home. The house is still, footsteps are gone, the bed feels wide, and rides to church feel heavy. After my loss, I expected the world to stop, at least briefly, but it didn't.

The same things that were required of me before April 12th were the same things, plus more, that were required of me afterward. Picking up where I left off was very difficult, and I learned the hard way that I couldn't go about life as if it were over for me. I had to do as David did in 1 Samuel 30:6 get up and figure out how to encourage myself in the Lord.

Death is not the end.
I am still here.

I can still be successful in anything I put my hands to. I am the same person, but now stronger, because I have had to weather a storm I wasn't prepared for. I am fearfully and wonderfully made. I deserve love, and I have plenty to give. Each day, my self-encouragement reflected my changing emotions—sometimes I felt motivated, other times weighed down by sorrow. Over time, I learned to navigate my new life after tragedy. Grief does not follow a traditional timeline, and everyone moves forward at their own pace. At some point, though I'm not sure exactly when, I noticed a shift within: the longing to connect, share companionship, give love, and be loved again began to feel real.

While I knew these feelings were not a sin against God, they brought confusion. Sometimes I felt betrayal, almost as if I were cheating on my husband. Realizing someone else wanted to know me beyond friendship or sisterhood in Christ created a tug-of-war inside me—my heart pulled between excitement and fear. The stress was constant: wanting love in one moment, rejecting it the next. I bore the weight of my real emotions, struggling to protect others' feelings and often ignoring my own.

Why did I do that?

No one ever made me feel as if I could not move forward in love. Yet I believed that because my husband was loved by so many people, I could not express feelings for another. I would disregard my feelings and torture myself with questions that were unfair to me.

Will our family and friends think I've moved on too soon?
Will my church feel I've forgotten our love story?

Will this decision hurt others?
Is my daughter old enough to understand?
Will she be okay?

Because of this war in my mind, I would begin relationships and then quietly slip out of them. I kept it so private that it often made the other person feel as if I wasn't ready to love again. I recall attending a revival one evening when a guest bishop, someone I had never met, openly prophesied a word into my life. To my knowledge, no one had spoken to him about me.

That night, he spoke into my life with a word straight from God. Just before I took my seat, he said, **"You shall marry again, saith the Lord."** At that moment, relief washed over me. I wanted to shout, *Thank you, Jesus, for considering me. The urge to cry followed quickly. Despite these strong emotions, I contained myself, remaining calm and composed as I returned to my seat.* In my mind, I worried that showing my feelings might seem disrespectful to the memory of my late husband. This internal conflict happened often. As the days grew longer and the nights lonelier, I slowly grew stronger and wiser. My boldness and desire to live free of others' opinions grew. I began telling myself, *"This is my life."*

When I stopped being angry with God and honestly shared my feelings, I realized I can't live for others' approval—no one will ever agree with me. I wish I'd known that wanting to love again wasn't disloyalty or weakness but healing. Others need time, but my heart deserves to heal.

Love after loss doesn't erase the past; it builds on it. Loving again doesn't mean loving my spouse less—our love shaped my capacity to love more deeply. Dating after loss wasn't about replacing Tony; he's irreplaceable. For me, it was about rediscovering myself with someone new.

It takes courage. It takes honesty. And it takes a willingness to be vulnerable again. During my journey of rediscovery, my emotions shifted rapidly: I felt joy one moment and sadness the next. There were times when I would laugh on a date, only to cry on the drive home, moving between hope for the future and grief for the past. My grief didn't end because I chose to open my heart to love again; it simply changed shape. Healing does not mean forgetting. It means you have made peace with your loss enough to allow your heart to open again, even with fresh scars. I loved my husband with my whole heart, and I had to remind myself, again and again, that I was still here. And while I am here, I deserve happiness. In time, those who truly love me will understand that choosing to love again is not a replacement for my late husband—it is simply the continuation of my journey. Being open to love again is a testament to the fact that love, even after loss, still has the final say.

To My Readers

You may have walked through the valley of the shadow of death, and yet here you stand. That alone is a testimony. You have faced a kind of heartbreak that could have silenced your spirit, but instead it has deepened it. And now you feel a stirring of love calling your name. Do not be afraid of this new beginning. Love did not die with the one you lost; it was planted deeper within you. The love you shared was never meant to end. It was meant to teach, to shape, and to prepare your heart for the fullness that still awaits. When God restores, He does not replace. He ***renews***.

He breathes new life into our broken places and reminds us that joy was not buried with our sorrow. So let this next chapter be written in faith, not fear. Let it be guided by gratitude, not guilt. What you once had was sacred. And what may still come can be sacred too. Trust that God is not finished writing your story. The same hand that carried you through the darkness will lead you into light again. When love finds you, whether quietly or suddenly, you can receive it without fear. Because God is love, and love always leads us forward, even through the shadows, to a brighter day.

Dating after loss is not about replacing the person you lost. It is about recognizing that your life is still unfolding and that companionship can still be part of your future. Approaching this new chapter with patience, honesty, and emotional awareness can help make the journey healthier and more meaningful.

Give Yourself Time to Heal

There is no universal timeline for when someone should begin dating again. Healing looks different for everyone. Some people feel ready sooner, while others need more time to process their grief and rediscover themselves as individuals.

Before entering a new relationship, it can be helpful to ask yourself whether you are emotionally ready to share your life with someone else. This does not mean your grief must be completely gone. Grief often remains in some form. But it is important to have reached a place where your desire for companionship comes from healing rather than loneliness alone.

Be Honest About Your Journey

Anyone entering your life after loss deserves honesty about where you are emotionally. Being open about your grief, your memories, and your healing process allows the relationship to grow from a place of understanding rather than confusion. A healthy partner will recognize that your past is part of your story and will respect the love you shared with your spouse. Honesty also helps you honor yourself. You do not need to pretend that your past never existed. The right person will understand that love does not erase previous love; it expands the heart's capacity.

Release Guilt About Loving Again

Guilt is common when widows open their hearts to new love, but loving again does not diminish past love. It is evidence of healing within you. Choosing to live fully does not betray your loved one.

Move at a Comfortable Pace

Dating after loss often comes with emotional ups and downs. There may be moments of excitement followed by moments of grief. You may laugh on a date and later feel overwhelmed with memories. This is part of the process. Allow yourself to move slowly. Take time to evaluate your feelings, communicate openly, and ensure that the relationship feels emotionally safe. There is no need to rush.

Trust God With the Process

For people of faith, dating again after loss can feel spiritually complicated. Questions about God's will, purpose, and timing often arise. It can be comforting to remember that God understands your heart completely. He knows your memories, your pain, and your hopes for the future. Bringing this part of your journey to Him in prayer can provide clarity and peace as you move forward. Trust that God can guide your steps, even in areas of life that feel uncertain. Opening your heart again is not a rejection of the past. It is a reflection of healing, courage, and the willingness to continue living the life God has given you.

A Prayer for Those Opening Their Heart Again

Heavenly Father,

You know the story of my heart. You have walked with me through moments of deep love and through the pain of losing someone who meant so much to my life. You saw the tears, the quiet prayers, and the long nights when I wondered how I would move forward. Today, I come before You with a heart that is learning how to live again. Lord, opening my heart to love again feels both hopeful and frightening. There are moments when I feel excited about the possibility of companionship, and other moments when fear and uncertainty rise within me. Help me navigate these emotions with wisdom and peace.

Remind me that loving again does not erase the love I once had. The memories I carry are still sacred, and the story of my life did not end with loss. Give me the courage to move forward without guilt. Teach me how to embrace healing while honoring the past. Help me trust that You are still guiding my steps, even in this new and unfamiliar season.

If love is part of the future you have prepared for me, lead me to someone who understands my journey, respects my story, and walks beside me with kindness and grace. Guard my heart from fear and fill it with peace. Help me move forward with patience, honesty, and faith in Your plan. Thank you for reminding me that my life still holds purpose, joy, and possibility. And if love finds me again, help me receive it as a gift, without shame or fear, and with gratitude.

In Jesus' name,
Amen.

CHAPTER 10

The Hurt Beneath Good Intentions

When I experienced loss, I quickly learned that grief doesn't just change you, it changes the people around you too. Suddenly, the air between us felt different. Conversations that once came easy turned heavy and hesitant. Many times, I could see and feel the discomfort in people's eyes as they searched for something to say. Some people said too much, offering church jargon or scriptures that sounded comforting on the surface but landed like stones.

"They're in a better place."

"At least they're not suffering."

"Everything happens for a reason."

"God has need of them."

Just to name a few.

Their words weren't cruel. They were just unsteady, sometimes premature, born out of a need to fill the silence that grief had created. Others said and did nothing. They stopped calling and stopped showing up, not because they stopped caring, but because they didn't know how to face or process my pain.

I think my grief made them afraid and uncomfortable, afraid of saying the wrong thing, or maybe afraid of what my loss reminded them of. But over time, I realized that most people simply aren't taught how to sit with sorrow. We live in a world that rushes healing, that treats grief like something to fix instead of something to carry together. In reality, grief is a natural and necessary part of the human experience, and it does not diminish our relationship with God. In my case, because I am a pastor, people assumed that the best way to support me was to throw out a scripture. However, in many moments, that was far from the truth.

It's not that quoting scripture was wrong, because God's Word never fails, for it is **a lamp unto my feet and a light unto my path** (Psalm 119:105).

But timing matters. In my culture, scriptures are sometimes weaponized by well-meaning but misguided individuals. They may use them to prescribe how a grieving person should cope or behave. People in pain have been told to simply "trust God" or "pray harder," without acknowledging the complex and deeply personal nature of grief. This can invalidate a grieving person's real emotions and struggles. It pushes them further into isolation and despair.

Ultimately, scripture is a source of wisdom and comfort, but it must be approached with humility, discernment, and a deep understanding of its context. It is essential to seek guidance from God the Father as to how you can help without causing offense.

Be led of the Lord instead of throwing out scriptures without thought, simply continuing a cultural habit that sometimes needs to be modified.

Church jargon can also be misused by those who unintentionally impose their beliefs or expectations on others. In the face of grief, some people use scriptures to preach judgment, condemnation, or divine reasoning, further compounding the pain already felt by the grieving person. It is essential not just to speak, but to listen—with an open heart, seeking to understand the right message in light of another person's experience and struggle. In the early days of my loss, my heart was raw, and every breath felt like effort. Even a verse of hope sometimes sounded like a rebuke instead of a reprieve.

Every time someone said, *"All things work together for good,"* my spirit ached, not because I didn't believe it, but because I was not ready to receive any other good other than what had been taken from my daughter and I.

When they said, *"Tony is in a better place,"* in my heart I screamed, *"But I want him here!"*

I even got offended by a loving brother who sent word to me that *"my latter would be greater."* I wept and said, *"But what was wrong with what I had God?"* Oh, so often I would hear the words, "Be strong."

But in my heart, I wanted to say, *"People, please... just be quiet. Right now, I just need permission to be true to how I feel in this moment."*

I know that people truly loved me and wanted nothing more than to offer comfort in their words. However, sometimes love requires silence more than scripture, and presence more than preaching. Jesus Himself wept at the tomb of Lazarus before He raised him. He didn't rush to fix the pain. He first entered into it. *(John 11:35)*

For me, the most powerful comfort didn't come from words at all. It came from presence. From someone sitting beside me, saying nothing, but staying close enough to remind me that I wasn't alone. I am grateful to the friends and family who let my tears fall without trying to stop them. I had many bouts of anger and often let them out at random moments.

One evening, my closest friends and family came over to help me pack up Tony's things so that they could be given to those he would have wanted to have as memorabilia. As I sat in my walk-in closet weeping through every item, my sorrow soon turned into rage. I began snatching clothes off the hangers, swinging, kicking and punching the clothes as if they were a live person. I remember that day like it was yesterday. The room cleared out quickly.

No one stopped me. No one yelled, "Tasha, calm down."

Everyone simply stood in the next room until I was finished. Afterward, everyone continued what they were doing as if nothing had happened. I left the room and went to sit in the car. My best friend followed me, opened the back door, and got into the car. She said, "Friend, I'm going to sit with you, and I promise I won't say a word."

Silence filled the air. Then with a quiet, gentle voice she whispered, "I know you're hurting, friend... but I didn't know you could fight like that."

I looked up in the rearview mirror, tears in my eyes, looking like Tina Turner after fighting Ike in that famous scene, and I laughed until my tears became tears of comfort. We slowly got out of the car, embraced, and walked back into the house to continue packing. When I got back in the room, the rest of the family noticed that my spirit had lifted. It opened the door for all of us to crack jokes and find space to laugh in a moment that minutes earlier felt so heavy. This was what I needed. I did not need someone telling me to be strong. In that moment, as I packed up what used to be a part of my life, I was overwhelmed with sadness and simply didn't know how to process it.

People who are grieving can be very sensitive, and even kind words can cut deeper than silence ever could. Now I'm not saying to be silent rather than speak, but I am saying to be led by the Lord and be authentic. If you don't know what to say, say that.

"Sis, I really don't know what to say. I'm honestly at a loss for words."

The thing about pain is that it doesn't always take motive into account. A wound is still a wound even when made with gentle hands. There are moments in grief when words fall short, and yet people—out of love, habit, or a desire to help—sometimes say things they haven't fully thought through. I remember one moment at my husband's memorial service before the funeral.

The bishops and clergy gathered in my church office to show their support for my church family and me. I became overwhelmed by the number of people who had traveled to support us, and the reality of everything hit me. I began to weep. One of the clergymen said,

"Bishop, can we take this time to pray for Pastor Tate?"

Our Bishop turned to me and asked,

"Did you ask for prayer?"

He then said to the audience in the room,

"She may not even want that right now."

Then he asked me a second time,

"Pastor Tate, do you want prayer?"

I replied softly,

"No, sir."

I am fully aware that prayer still unlocks doors and that its power can change atmospheres. We must remember that prayer can still be powerful even without an audience. All I wanted in that moment was space to process what was about to take place in my life. That moment spoke volumes about timing. He then began to educate the room about our words and the importance of timing. Grief can be uncomfortable, even for those who love you the most. Many days, I didn't know what I needed. I just knew what I didn't need. I discovered that people's presence didn't need to be perfect.

Sometimes the most healing words said to me were simply:

"I care."

Sometimes the holiest act was simply showing up, not with answers, but with empathy and patience. Healing does not happen in straight lines. Some days, I took steps forward. Some days, I stumbled backward.

Grief is not weakness.

It is simply love learning to navigate in new spaces. In times of grief, it is crucial to seek compassionate and empathetic support. Find those who can hold space for our pain without judgment or empty platitudes. It is important to allow ourselves to feel the full range of emotions that grief brings. Acknowledge the deep sense of loss and emptiness that comes with it. Grief makes every word feel louder, every silence feel heavier, and every well-meant gesture land in the wrong place.

And that's okay.

Allow grace to fill your heart. People around you often don't know the right things to say—or when to say nothing at all.

They fumble.

They rush.

They overstep.

They pull back too far.

Not because they don't care, but because they don't know how to walk the path, you're on and or have been accustomed to a tradition that has been passed down for generations. As confusing and painful as it can be, try to be patient. They are learning from you in this new season, the same way you are learning yourself. Their clumsy words may be the only way they know to show love. Their silence may come from fear of making things worse. Their eagerness to help you "move forward" may be their attempt to rescue you from pain they cannot bear to watch.

Be patient with them, not because your grief is small, but because your heart is big, and your pain is real. You don't owe anyone perfection, but you can give yourself the grace to step back, breathe, and remember that most people are trying even when it doesn't look or sound like it.

To the gracious helpers: Keep being authentic and remember to go before the Lord for guidance in the gift of helps.

Remember that not all help is good help. Grief can be awkward for everyone, so show grace even when the grieving person misinterprets your words or help. They want to receive it, but sometimes, hurting people hurt people. I learned this later in my grief journey. There were times I reacted sharply towards people that I believed were being insensitive. I responded in ways I would have never done before grief. The Holy Spirit would often convict me and encourage me to apologize and to also be patient with them and with myself. I had to realize that even in moments when it felt like no one truly understood the depth of what I was carrying, I was still surrounded by people who cared more than their words could express. As we all grow together, may you feel love in the small places, comfort in the quiet moments, and strength in knowing that your heart is doing its best.

Let's discuss some Statements that could be offensive and helpful to someone who is grieving.

When someone is grieving, many people want to help but struggle to find the right words. Out of love and discomfort, they may say things they believe will bring comfort. However, certain phrases, though well-intentioned, can unintentionally deepen the pain of someone who is already hurting. Understanding what not to say can help us respond with greater compassion and wisdom.

Below are some common phrases that grieving people often hear, along with gentler ways to offer support.

Instead of Saying:

"They're in a better place."

While this may be theologically comforting, it can sometimes feel dismissive to someone who deeply wishes their loved ones were still here.

Try Saying:

"I'm so sorry for your loss. I know how much they meant to you."

This statement acknowledges both the loss and the love that existed.

Instead of Saying:

"Everything happens for a reason."

For someone in deep grief, this statement can feel like an attempt to explain away their pain.

Try Saying:

"I can't imagine how difficult this must be, but I'm here for you."

This statement allows space for grief without forcing an explanation.

Instead of Saying:

"Be strong."

Grieving people often feel pressure to appear strong even when their hearts feel shattered.

Try Saying:

"You don't have to be strong right now. It's okay to feel whatever you're feeling."

Giving permission to feel weak can be incredibly healing.

Instead of Saying:

"At least they're not suffering anymore."

Although this may be true, these statements can minimize the emotional weight of loss.

Try Saying:

"I know how much you loved them. I'm so sorry you're going through this."

This statement validates the relationship and the depth of the loss.

Instead of Saying:

"You'll get through this."

While meant to encourage, this phrase can unintentionally rush someone's healing process. While minimizing the need to sometimes sit in the pain to deal with it.

Try Saying:

"I'll walk through this with you."

Grief is easier to carry when someone is willing to stay present.

Instead of Saying:

Nothing at All

Sometimes people avoid the grieving person completely because they fear saying the wrong thing.
However, silence through absence can feel like abandonment or isolation.

Try Saying:

"I honestly don't know what to say, but I care about you, and I'm here in whatever capacity you will allow me to be in".

Honesty and presence often speak louder than perfect words.

Instead of Saying:

"At least they lived a long life."

This statement tries to measure loss logically, but grief isn't logical.

Try saying:

"No amount of time ever feels like enough."
"Their life mattered so much.

This statement validates the love one has for their loved one.

Instead of Saying:

"I know exactly how you feel."

Grief is deeply personal—no two experiences are identical. This can frustrate someone if they don't agree.

Try saying:

"I think I can relate but I may not fully understand because I am not you, but I care about what you're going through. If you want to share how you feel, I'm here to listen."

This statement allows the love for their loved one to remain personal and allow one to feel supported in that love.

Instead of Saying:

"God needed another angel."

This statement can create confusion, anger, or Spiritual tension as God Don't NEED anything. He is God!

Try Saying:

"I'm praying for your comfort and peace. And may God hold you close during this time.

Taking that statement out altogether cuts down on the frustration of trying to figure out what God needed their loved one for.

Instead of Saying:

"You'll get over it."

Grief isn't something you "get over"—you learn to navigate life with the reality that your loved one will not be present.

Try Saying:

"Take all the time you need." I will keep you in my thoughts and prayers.

This statement allows one to grief properly without having to hide their true feelings.

Instead of Saying:

"At least you still have... (other children, spouse, etc.)"

This unintentionally replaces or compares the person who was lost. And diminishes their value in your life.

Try Saying:

"There's no replacing them." But I am here if and when you need me.

This statement validates the life of the loved one and does not diminish their existence.

Instead of Saying:

"Time heals all wounds."

Time doesn't erase loss—it just changes how it's carried.

Try Saying:

"Grief changes over time, but I know it doesn't just disappear."
"I'll walk with you through this, however long it takes."

This statement sets the expectation that the timeline for grief is not the same for everyone.

Instead of Saying:

"They wouldn't want you to be sad."

This statement can make people feel guilty for grieving.

Try Saying:

"Your love for them shows in your grief."
"It's okay to miss them deeply."

Instead of Saying:

"You're young—you can remarry / have more children."

This statement replaces a person with a possibility. And someone who was deeply loved cannot be replaced.

Try Saying:

"No one can replace who you lost."
"That relationship was unique and meaningful."

This statements puts respect and value on the loved one the has passed.

Instead of saying:

"It's been ___ months/years..."

Saying this suggests grief has an expiration date.

Try Saying:

"I know grief doesn't follow a timeline."
"How has your navigation process been for you?

This allows one to discuss their navigation and feel loved while doing it.

Instead of Saying:

"God won't give you more than you can handle."

Although biblically true one may not be at the place to comprehend this statement based on their pain. This can make one feel pressured to endure silently or appear strong.

Try Saying:

"This is a heavy burden—lean on God and others."
"You don't have to carry this alone.

This allows one to fee supported.

Instead of Saying:

"Just keep busy."

Avoidance isn't healing.

Try Saying:

"If you need distraction or rest, both are okay."
"What do you need today?"

This helps with balance in grief.

Instead of Saying:

"Call me if you need anything."

This puts the burden on the grieving person to reach out. And in MOST cases, reaching out will NOT happen.

Try Saying:

"I'll check in on you this week."(And actually CHECK IN)
"Can I bring you a meal or sit with you tomorrow?"(And actually follow through with the response)

Having friends and family be proactive in their support helps ensure grief does not cause one to isolate in their pain.

Instead of Saying:

"You have to be strong for your family."

This can put pressure on one to suppress personal grief and create emotional build up.

Try Saying:

"You're allowed to grieve too."
"Who's supporting you right now?"

Encouraging one to process their own grief allows one to heal properly.

A Simple Rule of thumb

When someone is grieving, discernment is paramount. Most are not looking for perfect solutions, theology, polished advice, or carefully constructed explanations. More often, they simply need presence, patience, compassion and consistency. Even a listening ear, a gentle embrace, or a quiet moment of shared silence can sometimes minister more deeply than a thousand carefully chosen words. When we approach grief with humility and love, we become vessels through which God can use to comfort the brokenhearted.

CHAPTER 11

A Legacy Set in Order

Legacy is not only what you leave behind. It is also what you leave within.

Scripture teaches us to face the realities of life with wisdom, not fear. *"Teach us to number our days, that we may gain a heart of wisdom"* (Psalm 90:12).

Numbering our days is not about counting down to the end of life. Rather, it is about living intentionally, loving deeply, and preparing faithfully. Preparing for the future is not a lack of faith; it is an expression of it. When you take responsibility for your affairs, you quietly tell your family, *I love you enough to plan ahead so that you do not have to carry this burden in your grief.*

A godly legacy is built through prayer, integrity, obedience, and trust in God. It is also built through wise preparation. Life insurance, a clear will, and thoughtful final directives are not cold or impersonal tasks. They are sacred acts of stewardship. These acts protect the people you love from confusion, financial strain, and painful decisions. Such decisions often come in moments of shock and sorrow. Leaving a legacy means leaving peace instead of chaos.

"For God is not a God of disorder but of peace" (1 Corinthians 14:33).

A will becomes a final letter of care. Life insurance provides stability, and a final directive offers clarity when clarity is hardest to find during grief. Through preparation, love extends beyond a lifetime. The Bible declares, *"A good person leaves an inheritance for their children's children"* (Proverbs 13:22).

That inheritance is not only financial. It is spiritual. It is wisdom. It is the example of a life lived responsibly before God. When your family watches you face mortality with faith rather than fear, they learn that trusting God and planning wisely can coexist in the same heart. Yet in many families, particularly in my culture, conversations about death feel forbidden.

Talking about death before its time can feel like inviting it, as if planning for death shows a lack of faith. So we avoid it. We whisper around it. We pretend it will not come. But avoidance does not protect our families. Only preparation does. Thoughtful planning allows loved ones to grieve without unanswered questions. It creates space for remembrance instead of regret. I did not fully understand this until loss became personal. Losing my husband was a painful experience, but one burden I did not have to carry was guessing what he would have wanted. We had many conversations about death. Sometimes they were serious. Sometimes they were joking. Often, they happened in rooms full of family members where the questions felt random or out of place.

"Who would you want to preach your eulogy?"

"If they cannot, who is your second choice?"

"What do you want to be buried in, or do you want cremation?"

These were some of the questions I would ask in the room. One day, my husband asked me, "Babe, if you die, do you care if I remarry?" I teased him and said, "Remarry if you want to, but if MJ calls her 'Mom,' I'm coming back with a vengeance." Laughter would fill the room. It seemed lighthearted. Almost unnecessary. But it wasn't. Those conversations were love in disguise.

When Tony passed away, the details of his homegoing services were clear. The financial responsibilities were manageable because he had planned well. In the middle of heartbreak, I was not scrambling to guess his wishes. He had already given me that gift. Even so, his passing opened my eyes to what we had not prepared for. We had not secured insurance that would have paid off the house. We assumed we had time. We thought hard work alone would carry us through. After he was gone, I realized how fragile those assumptions were. Suddenly, my mind filled with questions:

Who will care for my child if I leave too soon?
Who will handle my arrangements now that I am a widow?
How much life insurance is enough so my daughter never struggles?
Who receives the things that matter most to me?
Who will make decisions for me if I become ill?

I found myself praying and writing. I asked God for wisdom as I wrote my answers. I wanted my family to never have to wonder what I would have wanted. Love plans ahead. It says: *I will carry this responsibility now, so you will not have to carry it later.*

Here are simple, practical ways to do that:

Clearly outline how you want your assets distributed and name someone you trust to carry out your wishes.

Secure adequate life insurance.

Provide stability for your family. Cover funeral expenses, debts, and daily living needs.

Write your final directives.

Document your medical wishes and end-of-life decisions. This way, your loved ones are not forced to guess during emotional moments.

Organize important documents.

Keep policies, accounts, passwords, and legal papers together in one secure place. Make sure someone knows where to find them.

Have the hard conversations.

Speak your wishes out loud. Clarity brings peace and unity.

Pray over every decision.

Invite God into the process. *"Commit to the Lord whatever you do, and He will establish your plans"* (Proverbs 16:3).

These steps are not morbid. They are merciful. In making these preparations, you say one final time: *I still choose you. I still protect you even when I sleep in the Lord.*

Finishing well is not about perfection. It is about obedience and love carried through to the end. There should be deep joy in knowing that your preparation becomes a final blessing. Your legacy will live on beyond paperwork. It will live in the peace your family feels. In the burdens they did not have to carry. In the clarity you left behind. And in the faith you modeled. In their hardest moments, they will remember your care. On uncertain days, they will remember your wisdom. And when life feels overwhelming, they will see how your love prepared the way. That is a legacy set in order.

Scriptures About Legacy and Stewardship

The Bible reminds us that planning for the future and caring for our families are acts of wisdom and faith. These scriptures offer encouragement for those seeking to leave a meaningful and godly legacy.

Psalm 90:12

"Teach us to number our days, that we may gain a heart of wisdom."

Recognizing the value of time encourages us to live intentionally and make wise decisions for the future.

Proverbs 13:22

"A good person leaves an inheritance for their children's children."

Legacy extends beyond one generation. Wise preparation can bless families for years to come.

1 Timothy 5:8
"Anyone who does not provide for their relatives, and especially for their own household, has denied the faith."

Scripture emphasizes the importance of caring for our families with responsibility and foresight.

Proverbs 21:5
"The plans of the diligent lead surely to abundance."

Careful planning is not a lack of faith; it reflects diligence and wisdom.

Ecclesiastes 7:12
"Wisdom preserves those who have it."

Wisdom protects and guides both our present decisions and our future impact.

Proverbs 16:3
"Commit to the Lord whatever you do, and He will establish your plans."

Inviting God into our planning allows Him to guide our steps and strengthen the legacy we leave behind.

A Prayer for Leaving a Godly Legacy

Heavenly Father,

Thank You for the gift of life and for the people You have placed within my care. Every relationship, every responsibility, and every opportunity I have been given are blessings I do not take lightly.

Lord, help me live my life with wisdom and intention. Teach me to steward the time, resources, and relationships You have entrusted to me in a way that honors You.

Give me the courage to prepare for the future with faith rather than fear. Guide my decisions so that the legacy I leave behind reflects love, responsibility, and trust in You.

Help me care for my family well, not only in the words I speak today but also in the plans I make for tomorrow. May my preparation bring peace to those I love and remove burdens they should never have to carry alone.

More than anything, let my life be remembered for the faith I lived, the love I gave, and the example I set before others.

May the legacy I leave behind point people toward Your goodness and grace.

In Jesus' name, Amen.

CHAPTER 12

Death is not the end

Death is not the end, though it often feels like an ending when I stand in the silence it leaves behind.

Death can feel heavy, final, and absolute—like a door that has closed with no handle on the other side. It presses against the human heart and whispers the lie that this is where the story stops. It tries to convince me that the voice I loved is gone forever and that the presence I depended on has vanished into nothingness. Every life carries an expiration date, though none of us can see it written. We live, plan, build, and love as if time will always stretch ahead of us, yet God reminds us that our days are numbered by His wisdom, not our wishes.

Scripture says, ***"You have decided the length of our lives. You know how many months we will live, and we are not given a minute longer"*** (Job 14:5).

This truth can be difficult for the human heart to accept, because love always wants more time. We never reach a point where we feel finished loving the people God gave us. We want more conversations, more laughter, more ordinary days that we now know were never ordinary at all. But even when life feels cut short to us, it was never outside God's awareness or authority.

There is something within us that wishes the people we love could stay forever. We do not want our parents, our spouses, our siblings, or our friends to leave this earth. Love naturally resists separation. It was never part of God's original design for humanity to experience death, which is why death feels so unnatural and painful to the soul. Yet Scripture reminds us that our times are not random; they are held securely in God's hands.

David declared, ***"My times are in Your hands"*** (Psalm 31:15).

This means no life ends by accident. No moment is outside His control. God alone sees the full beginning and the full ending, and He alone knows when a life's earthly assignment has been fulfilled. Even Jesus acknowledged the divine timing of life and death.

Ecclesiastes 3:1–2 tells us, ***"To everything there is a season, a time for every purpose under heaven: a time to be born, and a time to die."***

Those words remind me that death is not a failure of life but the completion of a season God ordained. While I may wish for more time, God sees the eternal picture that I cannot see. He knows when the work is finished, when the race has been run, and when it is time to call His children home.

Psalm 139:16 says, ***"All the days ordained for me were written in your book before one of them came to be."***

This means nothing about my life, or the lives of those I love, has ever surprised God. This truth does not remove grief, but it gives grief somewhere to rest. It reminds me that the people I love were never truly mine to keep forever; they were entrusted to me for a season. When that season ends, they return to the One who gave them breath in the first place. The same God who decided their first breath also decides their last. Because He is loving, He is not careless with our lives. Because He is sovereign, He is not mistaken in His timing. And because He is eternal, death is never the end of the relationship, only the end of the earthly chapter.

Faith answers differently. Faith reminds me that death is not a period. It is a comma. It is not the end of the story, but a transition into a chapter with no ending. Scripture assures me, ***"To be absent from the body is to be present with the Lord"*** (2 Corinthians 5:8).

That means the very moment I feel the ache of goodbye on earth, heaven is already welcoming them home. What feels like loss here, is fullness there. What feels like silence here, is praise there. What feels like separation here, is a reunion there. Death does not erase the believer; it escorts them into the presence of God.

The Word of God reminds me that this life, as meaningful and fragile as it is, was never meant to be permanent.

"For here we have no continuing city, but we seek one to come" **(Hebrews 13:14).**

This earth was always temporary ground, and eternity was always the destination. Death is not destruction. It is crossing over. Jesus Himself reframed death in a way that removes its terror. When Lazarus died, Jesus said, ***"Our friend Lazarus sleeps"*** (John 11:11).

Sleep is not an ending. Sleep anticipates awakening. Sleep assumes restoration. Sleep carries the promise that what appears over is only waiting for movement again. Jesus intentionally used this language to show that death does not have ultimate authority. Death cannot permanently hold what belongs to God. There will be a day when the trumpet sounds, for Scripture declares:

***"For the Lord Himself will descend from heaven with a shout... and the dead in Christ will rise first. Then we who are alive and remain shall be caught up together with them... and thus we shall always be with the Lord"* (1 Thessalonians 4:16–17).**

Together. That word settles deeply into my spirit. Not separated forever. Not lost eternally. Together again. Death interrupts proximity, but it cannot sever the covenant. Death pauses presence, but it cannot destroy love. Love does not originate in flesh; it originates in God.

***"We love because He first loved us"* (1 John 4:19).**

And what God creates, death cannot erase. Yet even with this promise, the human heart still wrestles with fear. People fear death because it represents the unknown. It confronts the limits of human control. It removes the familiarity of what we can see and replaces it with what must be trusted. Ecclesiastes 3:11 says that God has ***"set eternity in the human heart."*** That means there is something within us that knows we were created to live beyond this life. But when eternity approaches, the flesh trembles because it cannot fully comprehend what the spirit already knows.

Fear also comes from separation. Death removes people from the arms of those who love them, and the human heart was not designed for separation; it was designed for connection. Death feels like theft because it takes what was visible and makes it invisible. It takes what was audible and makes it silent. It takes what was tangible and makes it untouchable. There is also the fear of unfinished purpose.

The quiet questions linger in the human soul:

Did I do enough?
Did I love enough?
Did my life matter?

Scripture acknowledges this reality when it says, ***"It is appointed for man to die once, but after this the judgment"*** (Hebrews 9:27).

The awareness of accountability can make death feel intimidating. But Jesus came specifically to break the power of that fear. Hebrews 2:14–15 explains that through His death, Jesus destroyed the one who had the power of death and freed those who had all their lives been held in slavery by their fear of dying.

Fear loses its grip when I understand that death no longer leads to condemnation for those who belong to Christ.

***"There is now no condemnation for those who are in Christ Jesus"* (Romans 8:1).**

Death is no longer a courtroom for the believer. It is a doorway home. The resurrection of Jesus permanently transformed death. When the tomb could not hold Him, it proved that death does not have the authority to hold those who are His. Scripture proclaims, ***"Death has been swallowed up in victory. O death, where is your sting?"* (1 Corinthians 15:54–55).**

The sting of death was sin, and Jesus removed that sting through His sacrifice. Death may still bring sorrow, but it no longer brings defeat. It may still bring tears, but it no longer brings despair. Even Jesus wept at the grave of Lazarus (John 11:35), not because death had ultimate power, but because grief is the natural language of love interrupted. My grief does not mean my faith is weak.

My grief means my love was real. And love, when rooted in God, is never wasted. Love continues beyond the grave because God Himself is eternal. This is why we should not grieve without hope. Scripture does not command me not to grieve. It simply reminds me that my grief is different.

***"We do not grieve as others do who have no hope"* (1 Thessalonians 4:13).**

My tears carry expectation. My sorrow carries promise. My goodbye carries the certainty of reunion. His life guarantees mine. His resurrection guarantees theirs. His victory becomes my assurance. Until that day, I continue to live.

I carry forward what they poured into me. I honor their impact by the way I love, the way I serve, and the way I walk with God. Their absence shapes me, but it does not destroy me. Their departure reminds me that eternity is real and that heaven is not just a theological idea but a prepared place. Jesus promised, ***"I go to prepare a place for you... I will come again and receive you to Myself; that where I am, there you may be also"*** (John 14:2–3).

That promise removes the finality of death. Death may close my eyes here, but it opens them there. It may separate me from what is temporary, but it unites me with what is eternal. It may interrupt my earthly story, but it completes my eternal one.

To My Precious Readers

Grief has a way of teaching the heart things it never expected to learn. It teaches us that love is deeper than we realized. It reveals how profoundly our lives were shaped by the people who walked beside us. And it reminds us that the moments we once considered ordinary were often the most sacred. Losing someone we love changes the landscape of life. The rooms feel quieter. The routines feel unfamiliar. Even the laughter we once shared echoes differently in memory.

Yet grief also reveals something powerful. Love does not disappear simply because someone is no longer physically present. The love we shared continues to live within us—in the lessons they taught, the kindness they showed, and the ways they shaped who we have become. In many ways, the people we lose leave pieces of themselves within our lives. Their words guide us. Their faith strengthens us. Their memories comfort us. And slowly, over time, grief begins to transform.

The sharp pain of loss softens into remembrance. Tears begin to carry gratitude alongside sorrow. The silence that once felt unbearable begins to hold quiet moments of peace. We learn that healing does not mean forgetting. It means learning how to carry love differently. Faith reminds us that this life is not the final chapter of our story. Scripture often speaks of eternity not as a general idea but as a promise. The same God who breathed life into humanity has prepared a place beyond this world where sorrow, death, and separation no longer exist. Because of that promise, grief does not have the final word.

Hope does.

One day, every tear will be wiped away. The questions that trouble our hearts will be answered, and the reunions we long for will finally arrive. Until that day comes, we continue living. We love the people around us. We cherish the memories we carry. We honor the legacy of those who came before us. And when grief whispers that everything has ended, faith gently reminds us that the story is still unfolding. Night may fall, and sorrow may linger for a season, but the promise of God remains steady.

Morning is coming. And when that morning arrives, we will see clearly what faith has held onto all along: Death was never the end. It was only a matter of waiting until morning came. When the fear of death tries to rise within you, remember that death has limits. It cannot steal our souls. It cannot erase God's promises. And it cannot cancel what God has already made eternal.

It is the moment when faith becomes sight, hope becomes reality, and we step from what was temporary into what was always permanent. Though it may feel like a loss here, heaven declares it as an arrival. Though it may feel like goodbye here, God calls it a homecoming. And as I close, allow me to remind you, just as I remind my own heart, that when we live a life that is pleasing to God, we will see our loved ones again. This is not wishful thinking. This is the promise of God.

A Final Prayer for Those Grieving

Heavenly Father,

You are the God who sees every tear and hears every silent cry. You understand the places in our hearts that feel broken, the memories that rise without warning, and the longing that grief leaves behind.

Today, we come before You carrying the weight of loss.

For those who have buried a spouse, a parent, a child, a sibling, or a dear friend, we ask that Your presence meet them in the quiet spaces where sorrow lives. Wrap your peace around their hearts in moments when loneliness feels overwhelming. Remind them that even in their darkest hours, they are never alone.

Lord, grief can feel confusing and heavy. Some days bring strength, while other days bring waves of sadness that seem impossible to explain. In those moments, help us remember that healing is a journey and that Your grace meets us every step of the way.

Comfort those who are struggling to understand why their loved one was taken so soon. Bring reassurance to hearts that wrestle with unanswered questions. When the pain feels too deep for words, let Your presence speak where language fails.

Help us remember the love that was shared and the memories that still live within us. Let those memories become reminders of the blessings we experienced rather than only the pain of what was lost.

Teach us how to move forward with courage, knowing that grief and hope can exist in the same heart. Restore joy where sorrow once lived, and renew strength in those who feel weary.

Remind us that death is not the end of the story. Because of Your promise, we know that separation is temporary and that one day we will be reunited with those who have gone before us in faith.

Until that day, help us live with purpose, love deeply, and trust in the future You are still unfolding. Thank You for being our refuge in sorrow, our comfort in grief, and our hope beyond this life.

In Jesus' name,

Amen.

CHAPTER 13

The Benediction

Grief does not play fair, but the weapon of our warfare is not carnal. May you never forget how powerful prayer is in the time of Grief and trouble. I will end with a few prayers to help you in times of grief.

A Prayer for PEACE

Father God,

You are not the author of confusion — You are the Prince of Peace. And Your Word declares in John 14:27, "Peace I leave with you, the peace I give unto you: not as the world giveth." Lord, we are not asking for temporary relief. We are asking for your peace.

The kind that holds a grieving heart together
when everything familiar has fallen apart.

You said in Isaiah 26:3 that You will keep in perfect peace the one whose mind is stayed on You. So steady our minds, Lord. When grief replays memories on a loop... when silence feels loud... when tears come without warning... anchor our thoughts in You.

Your Word promises in Philippians 4:7 that Your peace will guard our hearts and our minds in Christ Jesus. Stand guard over us. Protect us from bitterness. Protect us from despair. Protect us from the lie that we will never feel joy again.

You said in Psalm 34:18 that You are near to the brokenhearted. Jesus, we ask You to draw near now. Sit beside every person reading this book who feels hollow, heavy, and undone.

We declare that grief will not steal our rest, our sanity, or silence our faith.
It will not steal our sanity.
and it will not silence our faith.

We receive Your peace — not fragile peace — but the peace that surpasses all understanding.

It is in the Mighty name of Jesus we pray,
Amen.

A Prayer for PURPOSE

Lord,

Loss can make it feel like the story ended too soon. Like something sacred was interrupted.

But Your Word says in Romans 8:28 that You work all things together for good — and that includes this pain. We may not understand it, but we trust that You are still working behind the scenes.

You declared in Jeremiah 29:11 that You know the plans You have for us — plans for hope and a future. God, we stand on that promise.

Our future did not die with our loss.

Shift us from asking "Why me?" to asking, "What now, Lord?"
Show us how to carry love forward.
Show us how to let this wound produce wisdom.
Show us how to turn mourning into mission.

Your Word says in Joel 2:25 that You can restore the years the locust has eaten. We are asking for restoration from what grief may have devoured. Restore vision. Restore clarity. Restore courage.

If we must walk through this valley, let us walk out refined and not ruined.

We declare that our pain and tears will not be wasted or meaningless, and this chapter will not cancel our calling.
Our tears will not be meaningless.
And this chapter will not cancel our calling.

It is in your matchless, majestic, and Strong name of Jesus we pray.

Amen.

A Prayer for POWER

Father,

We may be grieving — but we are not defeated.

Your Word says in 2 Timothy 1:7 that You have not given us a spirit of fear, but of power, love, and a sound mind. We reject fear right now in the name of Jesus. We reject hopelessness. We reject the lie that we will never be whole again.

You said in 2 Corinthians 12:9 that Your grace is sufficient, and Your strength is made perfect in weakness. God, when we feel weak, help us know that Your strength is about to show up.

You declared in Isaiah 40:31 that those who wait on You shall renew their strength — they shall mount up with wings like eagles.

Break every chain grief tries to wrap around our future. Because according to John 8:36, whoever the Son sets free is free indeed.

Death may have changed our lives, but it did not cancel our anointing, erase our assignment, or strip us of authority.
But it did not cancel our anointing.
It did not erase our assignment.
It did not strip us of authority.

The same power that raised Jesus from the dead lives in us — just as Romans 8:11 declares.

We will rise, breathe, love again, live again, walk in peace, move in purpose, and stand in power.
We will breathe.
We will love again.

We will live again.

And we will walk in peace.
We will move with purpose.
We will stand in power.

In Jesus' mighty name,
Amen.

Final Benediction

May the Lord bless you and keep you, just as Numbers 6:24–26 declares.
May He make His face shine upon you in your darkest hour.
May He be gracious to you when grief feels heavier than your faith.
And may He give you peace.

As you walk forward from these pages, may the God who is close to the brokenhearted hold you steady. (Psalm 34:18)

May He strengthen you with might by His Spirit in your inner being (Ephesians 3:16).
May He remind you that weeping may endure for a night, but joy still comes in the morning. (Psalm 30:5).

May every chain that wrapped itself around loosen its hold.
May every tear you have cried water the ground of your becoming.
May every valley you've walked through reveal a deeper revelation of who God is.

May you have peace that guards your heart.

Purpose that pulls you forward.
Power that reminds you of who you are.

And when the weight feels heavy again — because sometimes it will — may you remember that the same Spirit that raised Jesus from the dead lives in you. (Romans 8:11).

You are not abandoned, forgotten, or finished.
You are not forgotten.
You are not finished.

Loss may have changed your story.
But God is still writing.

So, rise in peace.
Walk with purpose.
And stand in power.

Amen.

ABOUT THE AUTHOR

Pastor NaTasha Harris-Tate was born in Milford, Delaware, to her parents, Jack Wanzer and Pastor Celestine Woodall. She accepted Christ at the young age of six and received her call to ministry at just 15 years old. By the age of 18, she was licensed and ordained in the office of an Evangelist.

With over 30 years in ministry, Pastor NaTasha has traveled across the country, sharing the Gospel through both song and preaching, boldly declaring that Jesus is the answer for the world today. Her life has been marked by a deep commitment to serving God and impacting lives through the power of His Word.

On April 26, 2014, she married the love of her life, Pastor Tony Tate Jr., and on November 27, 2017, they were blessed with a beautiful daughter, Moriah Joi. On August 25, 2018, Pastor NaTasha was ordained as Assistant Pastor of Penuel Tabernacle of Praise. Following the untimely passing of her husband, she stepped into the role of Senior Pastor, faithfully continuing the legacy they built together. A true worshipper at heart, Pastor NaTasha has a passion for ushering people into the presence of God through praise and worship. She is devoted to seeing lives transformed by the power of the Almighty and strives to walk in holiness as an example to others. God uses her mightily as she operates in the gifts of prophecy and healing, carrying a strong mantle of deliverance.

Pastor NaTasha remains committed to fulfilling the divine assignment on her life, anchored in her life scripture, Philippians 1:6: *"Being confident of this very thing, that He which hath begun a good work in you will perform it until the day of Jesus Christ."*

She has studied at Garry Westone Bible College in Wilmington, Delaware, and Sankofa Bible Institute at Oblate Bible College and Seminary in San Antonio, Texas. Pastor NaTasha's greatest desire is to remain an instrument of honor, skillfully used by the Master to edify the Body of Christ.

www.ingramcontent.com/pod-product-compliance
Lightning Source LLC
LaVergne TN
LVHW010950110826
845149LV00015B/3281

* 9 7 9 8 9 9 5 1 7 2 2 3 9 *